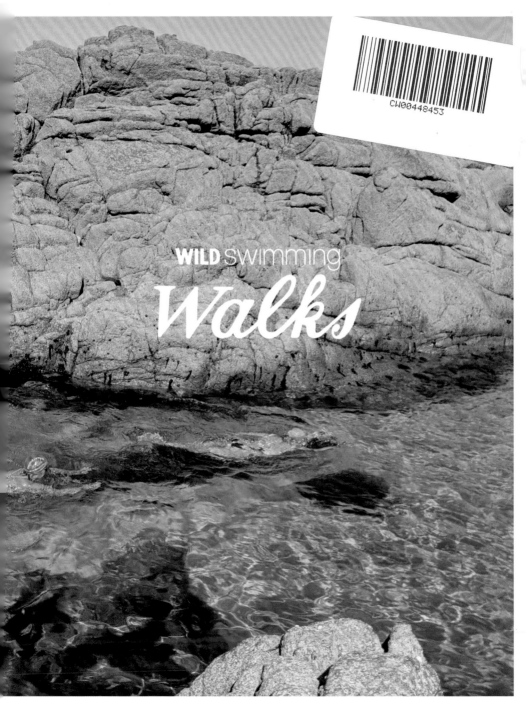

WILD swimming
Walks

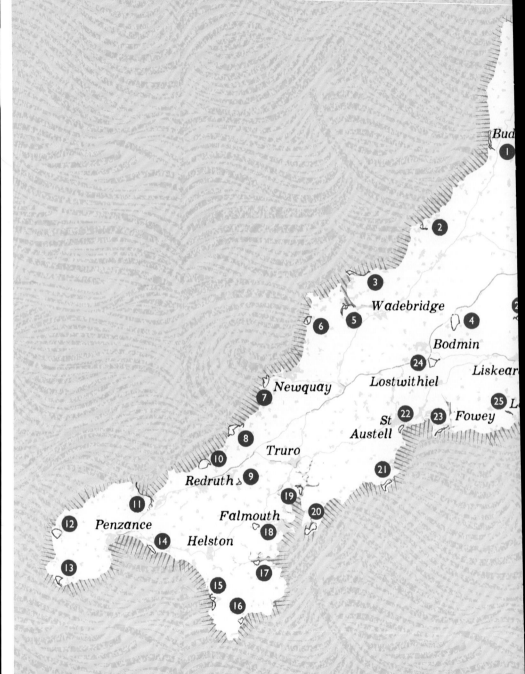

Bud

1

2

3

Wadebridge

5

6

4

Bodmin

Liskear

24

Lostwithiel

Newquay

7

22

23

Fowey

25 L

St
Austell

8

Truro

10

21

9

Redruth

19

11

20

Falmouth

12

Penzance

18

14

Helston

13

17

15

16

THE WALKS

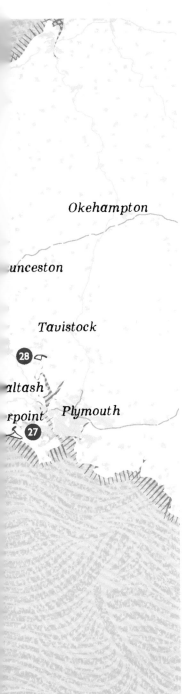

TABLE OF WALKS

No.	NAME	SWIMMING
1	Northcott Mouth and Bude Circular	Sea at Bude and Northcott Mouth beaches, tidal pools: Bude Sea Pool and Tommy's Pit
2	St Nectan's Glen and Bossiney Haven Circular	Sea at Bossiney Haven, waterfalls at St Nectan's Glen, river pools at Rocky Valley
3	Pentire, Lundy Hole and Port Quin Circular	Sea at Pentireglaze Haven, unnamed cove, Sandinway Cove, Lundy Bay, Port Quin
4	Cardinham Moor Lakes Circular	Burnt Heath Quarry Pool, Glynn Valley Quarry pool
5	Little Petherick Creek Circular	Sea at estuary beaches of Oldtown Cove, Dennis Cove and Little Petherick Creek
6	Trescore Islands Circular	Beaches at Porthcothan, lagoon at Trescore Islands, beach at Porth Mear
7	Holywell Bay and St Cuthbert's Well Circular	Beaches at Holywell Bay, Porth Joke and Vugga Cove
8	St Agnes and Chapel Porth Circular	Beaches at Trevellas Porth, Trevaunance Cove and Chapel Porth
9	Carn Marth Quarries Circular	Two quarry pools at Carn Marth
10	Portreath and Tehidy Country Park Circular	Sea at Portreath, tidal pool and Lady Basset's baths at Portreath
11	St Ives Steam and Swim	Sea at Porthmeor, Porthgwidden, Bamaluz, Harbour Porthminster and Porth Kidney beaches
12	St Just Circular	Sea at Porth Nanven, Priests Cove, Porth Ledden, tidal pool at Priests Cove
13	Porthgwarra and Nanjizal Circular	Sea at Porthgwarra Cove and Nanjizal Bay, tidal Pool and arch at Nanjizal
14	Perranuthnoe and Prussia Cove Circular	Sea at Perran Sands, Trevean Cove, Stackhouse Cove, Bessy's Cove
15	Mullion Figure of Eight	Sea at Poldhu Cove, Polurrian Cove, Mullion Cove
16	Poltesco and Cadgwith Circular	Sea at Poltesco and Cadgwith Coves, swim safari to collapsed sea cave: The Devil's Frying Pan
17	Frenchman's Creek Circular	Estuary beach at Penarvon Cove and Frenchman's Creek
18	Mabe Quarry Circular	Quarry pool at Spargo Downs
19	Trelissick Figure of Eight	Estuary and creek beaches at Trelissick, South Wood, Lamouth Creek and Roundwood Quay
20	St Anthony Head Circular	Sea at Towan, Little and Great Molunan beaches, estuary at Cellars Beach and Place Quay
21	Gorran Haven Circular	Sea at Gorran Haven, Vault and Hemmick beaches, swimming off rocks at Maenease Point
22	Charlestown Circular	Sea at Charlestown, Duporth and Porthpean; longer swims between the three beaches
23	Readymoney Beach to Polridmouth Figure of Eight	Sea at Readymoney and Polridmouth Coves
24	Lanhydrock Circular	Five pools on the upper River Fowey
25	Looe Estuary Adventure	Swim with outgoing tide down West Looe River. sea at Looe Town Beach
26	Minions to Goldiggins Quarry Circular	Freshwater pools at Goldiggins Quarry and Pony Pool
27	Portwrinkle and Sheviock Circular	Sea at Portwrinkle, tidal river at St Germans river
28	Cotehele and Tamar Swoosh	Estuary at Calstock; swim from Calstock to Cotehele Quay with outgoing tide

TERRAIN	REFRESHMENTS EN ROUTE	MILES	DIFFICULTY
Clifftops, urban and beaches	Cafés in Bude	4	Easy
Cliffs, fields, woods, steep climbs	Café at St Nectan's Glen	3.5	Medium
Cliffs, fields, steep climbs	None	9	Hard
Moorland, climbs, indistinct paths	None	6	Hard
Smooth track, fields, climbs, creekside	None	6.5	Medium
Cliffs, beaches, climbs, fields	Café in Porthcothan	3.5	Easy
Cliffs, beaches, climbs, fields	Cafés at Holywell Bay and Crantock)	5.5	Medium
Cliffs, coast path, moorland, lanes, steep climbs	Cafés at Trevaunance Cove and Chapel Porth	8.5	Hard
Fields, moorland, lanes	None	3.5	Easy
Cliffs, fields, woods, lanes, steep climbs	Cafés at Portreath	5.5	Hard
Town, cliffs, coast path, lanes, roads	Cafés in St Ives	7.5	Hard
Lanes, cliffs, coast path, climbs	Cafés in St Just and Cape Cornwall	5	Medium
Cliffs, coast path, steep climbs, fields	Café at Porthgwarra	4.5	Medium
Coast path, cliffs, climbs, fields, lanes	Café at Perranuthnoe	4	Easy
Coast path, steep climbs, fields, lanes	Cafés at Poldhu Beach and Mullion Cove	6.5	Hard
Lanes, coast path, climbs, cliffs, fields	Cafés at Cadgwith	3	Easy
Village lanes, fields, creekside	Cafés at Helford	3	Easy
Lanes, fields and rough tracks	None	3	Easy
Fields, woods, climbs, lanes	Café at NT Trelissick	5	Medium
Cliffs, coast path, woods, lanes	Café at Porth	6	Medium
Cliffs, coast path, fields, lanes	Café at Gorran Haven	5	Medium
Cliffs, lanes, fields, coast path, climbs	Cafes at Charlestown	3	Easy
Urban, lanes, cliffs, fields, climbs	Cafes at Fowey	5.5	Medium
Woods, climbs, riverbanks, tracks	Café at Lanhydrock	5	Medium
Woods, tracks, riverside	Cafés in Looe	2	Easy
Moorland, tracks, climbs	Cafés in Minions	4	Easy
Fields, road, lanes, woods, steep climbs	Café in Portwrinkle	8	Hard
Lanes, woods, fields and climbs	Cafés at Cotehele Quay and Calstock	4.5	Medium

Pentire Head, Polzeath

INTRODUCTION

"It is magic that comes leaping into the mind when we think of Cornwall, and in truth it is a magic place. Saints and legends, holy wells and ancient crosses, are everywhere… and at times there is an eeriness in this grim rock-bound coast, so that unadventurous people do not always feel easy in its presence. Certainly Cornwall is no place for the man who has no mystery. Here if anywhere it is plain that we are such stuff as dreams are made of."

From *Cornwall, England's Farthest South*
by Arthur Mee 1937

Cornwall. Kernow. A country, not a county, a kingdom with its own language and fierce identity. A place of romance, beauty and legend, but one whose people have historically had tough lives, battling both the sea and the land in their main industries of fishing, mining and farming. Around four million tourists visit every year, drawn mostly to the 300 miles of breathtaking coastline, but there is so much more to experience along Cornwall's central 'backbone', from magnificent moorland with ancient stone circles and quarry lakes to the china clay district, where the heaps of white spoil thrust skywards like Cornish Alps.

The Cornish identity is distinguished by separation and the proud independence of the men and women of the soil and the sea. The 'Corn' comes from the Cornish 'kern' meaning 'horn', and Cornwall is very nearly an island, with 80% of it surrounded by water, while you are never more than 16 miles from the coast. It has the sea on three sides and the Tamar forming a natural boundary with Devon for over 57 miles before it flows into the English Channel.

Cornwall is Celtic, with its own language, which after nearly dying out is thriving today; hence the 'Kernow a'gas dynergh' or 'Welcome to Cornwall' sign you will see as you drive over the River Tamar. Many people do not like it being called a county. Merv Davey, a former Grand Bard of Gorsedh Kernow, writes: "The term 'county' fails to recognise Cornwall's distinctive identity and encourages our friends in the media to fade Cornish identity into an amorphous 'Westcountry'. Many English counties have a strong sense of identity with rich traditions that contribute to the modern culture of these islands. I am not saying that Cornwall's culture is stronger or superior, simply that it belongs to the Cornish world and not the English one and to call it an English county betrays this identity."

You might argue, what does it matter? But this desire not to be an English county tells us something about the nature of Cornwall. That sense of independence has its roots in the geography of the place and its connections to the ancient Celtic world, on the routes between Ireland, Wales and Brittany. And of course, being at the end of a peninsula, it has long been far removed from the centre of power and government.

Today, Cornwall relies heavily on tourism to provide jobs and bring in money, and is officially the UK's favourite holiday destination, an accolade it wins year after year. Its main selling point is its spectacular coast, but it also has an irresistible aura of myth and mystery. The legend of King Arthur and the Knights of the Round Table is one that is ingrained into our national DNA, and Cornwall lays claim to it in places such as Tintagel and Dozmary Pool. There is even an Avalon app you can download, with a map to help you 'walk in the trail of King Arthur's footsteps'.

A little booklet called 'Cornish Legends', published in the 1960s, contains all manner of

Cornish folklore, from pixies to giants, ghost ships to miners' imps, and witches to wish hounds. Stories including the Spectre Ship of Porthcurno, the Witches of the Logan Stone, and the Giant of Nancledry convey the spirit of fable that permeates the Cornish experience. And again, like the spirit of independence, this goes back to the landscape. In the rolling mists coming in off the sea, great standing stones and stone circles, huge tors, and sea stacks and caves where the water foams and spurts, you can see the inspiration for these stories. And that legendary landscape endures today, for us all to explore and enjoy.

It is a swimmer's paradise. The south coast is sheltered from the prevailing south-westerly winds, providing safe, calm waters in many creeks and harbours that are perfect for swim safaris. From the gin-clear sea of Mevagissey Bay, to the languid green waters of the Helford River, this coast provides a warm welcome. The Lizard and Land's End have dramatic shorelines with imposing rocky buttresses as an exciting visual backdrop, and many caves, arches, tunnels and islands to explore. Inland,

the Cornish rivers are small but enticing, and there are spectacular freshwater quarries, the legacy of mining and quarrying on the moors. The north coast has rolling surf, rugged cliffs and many tidal pools, and the walks are just breathtaking.

This truly is a place you can have all manner of aquatic adventures. Whether it's swooshing down one of the many estuaries and creeks with the tide, swimming from beach to beach, or wallowing in the abundance of tidal pools, marvelling at the wildlife below the surface, you will find Cornwall an aquatic Avalon full of swimming surprises.

Delectable Duchy

The golden and unpeopled bays
The shadowy cliffs and sheep-worn ways
The white unpopulated surf
The thyme-and-mushroom scented turf
The slate-hung farms, the oil-lit chapels
Thin elms and lemon-coloured apples…

Sir John Betjeman – 1974

Porthmeor Beach, St Ives

River Fowey, Lanhydrock

Porthpean

THE COLOUR OF WATER

There are dozens of words to describe the colour of water, from turquoise and jade, to azure, emerald and aquamarine. And in our adventures around Cornwall, we think we have seen them all. Nowhere else have we found ourselves exclaiming "look at the colour of that water!" on so many walks. The vibrant, almost glowing colours are straight from a screensaver and are eminently Instagrammable. It's why collating the pictures for this book has been such a joy. We have swum in the former china clay pools of Cardinham Moor, where the milky sands turn the waters opal. We dipped in the liquid bliss of the upper Fowey, where mineral deposits glitter in the dappled indigo waters, like mythical pisky dust. We have shrieked with cold and with laughter under the sacred waterfall at St Nectan's Glen, as the cerulean-tinged white water thunders down, the spray refracting into a spectacular array of colours. However, it has been the different colours of the sea that have left us most in awe of Cornwall.

Cornwall itself is geologically tilted, which is why the north coast boasts mighty cliffs and deep slate blue water, while the southern shore is often sandy with shallow clear waters. A variety of factors leads to the remarkable palate of blues you will discover. Cornwall has very few rivers to wash mud and silt into the seas, meaning calm weather results in extraordinary water clarity. Heavy sand particles and a lack of sediment give the waters of west Cornwall an incredible turquoise colour. Sea beds made up of crushed shells give rise to cobalt blue and aquamarine, with the colours changing depending on the light, the depth of the water and time of day. Direct light from the sun can cause a different shade of blue from light that is diffused through clouds and mist or reflected when it bounces off the surface of the water. A week's holiday can take you through a diverse colour chart of blues, with no two days the same.

Trevellas Porth

The astonishing light and the exceptional water colours have inspired generations of artists to adopt Cornwall as their home. It was perhaps J.M. Turner who first highlighted the magnificent light and intense colours of Cornwall in his 1811 illustrated travel guide, *Picturesque Views on the Southern Coast of England*. His watercolour, oil and pencil sketches of Newlyn, St Ives and Penzance turned these sleepy towns into meccas for artists. By the 1930s, they had become a hive of creativity for bohemian painters and sculptors, inspired by the beautiful coastline around them.

Today, Cornwall continues to attract artistic types, with the late Barbara Hepworth saying of her home in St Ives: "The horizontal line of the sea and the quality of light and colour… reminds me of the Mediterranean light and colour, which so excites one's sense of form." We think that this is perhaps selling her adopted home a little short, and that there is hopefully another artist in the Mediterranean who is saying that the coastline there reminds them very much of Cornwall.

ENTERING THE LANDSCAPE

The popularity of wild swimming has grown enormously since we first started writing books about it almost a decade ago. Not that we take any credit for it, the word just got around! This is fantastic news, as the health benefits, both anecdotal and now scientifically proven, are huge. Not only is it great for your heart and circulation, it is apparently also good for your libido, while the natural high is undeniable. We've also heard that it is supposed to help weight loss, although we have always successfully countered this with the amount of cake we eat following a dip. It is also immensely beneficial for your mental health and we can vouch for this from personal experience. It certainly helps to reduces stress, anxiety and depression and can be very meditative. We've often joked that if a pharmaceutical company could find a way to bottle it, they would make a fortune.

There is also a real sense of community with wild swimming, and we are eternally grateful for the many lovely and like-minded friends we have met along the way. This book was put together with the help of many people who joined us throughout a year of research. They shared their enthusiasm, knowledge, photography skills, humour and cake as we traipsed all over Cornwall, falling even more in love with the county along the way. Sometimes things went wrong and we got hopelessly lost, or were sucked into bogs or arrived at potential swim spots that had dried up years before. But even the disasters were part of the fun, thanks to the wonderful people wild swimming seems to attract.

Another tremendous benefit of walking and swimming is that it allows you to reconnect with nature, the importance of which can never be underestimated. By enjoying nature we value and understand it more and want to do everything

Rocky Valley

Vault Beach, Gorran Haven

in our power to protect it. It's why we are really appreciative of the National Trust, which own a quarter (742 miles) of the 3,000-mile coastline of England, Wales and Northern Ireland. Alongside the South West Coast Path (England's longest nature trail), it ensures that we continue to have access to endless swim spots along the 300 miles of the Cornish coast. And it's why we don't mind throwing a few quid into a car park machine.

Of course, we have a responsibility to respect the places we are walking and swimming through, and also to educate the next generation to value the privilege and fragility of nature. As the popularity of wild swimming has grown, there has been a bit of a backlash with people not wanting to share swim spots, like territorial surfers protecting their secret breaks. And there is a balance to be struck. The collapse of society's engagement with nature is happening simultaneously with the collapse of the natural world. It's why National Parks only promote some car parks and sacrifice certain 'honeypots' for the greater good, knowing that most people don't venture very far from their vehicles.

"The thought that most of our children will never swim among phosphorescent plankton at night, will never be startled by a salmon leaping, a dolphin breaching, the stoop of a peregrine, or the rustle of a grass snake is almost as sad as the thought that their children might not have the opportunity."

George Monbiot

When deciding what swim walks to include in this book, we also felt a responsibility to ensure we weren't adversely impacting on nature by sending people to sensitive and fragile habitats. With this in mind, we eliminated places where we thought the environmental impact may be too great, including delicate riverbanks. We also excluded some quite well known spots because the Cornwall

Wildlife Trust and other organisations felt that wild swimming could have an adverse effect on the wildlife in that area. Many of the swims are from beaches and rocky outcrops, or harbours and quays where you can enter the water without damaging the banks. We have also updated our Wild Swimming Code in this book, so we can all pledge to protect the very environment we enjoy so much.

By not just driving directly to swim spots, but including circular walks as well, we can all enjoy the nature around us, whilst entering the landscape ourselves. We have also learnt about the natural and social history of Cornwall and all sorts of fascinating history along the way. With this in mind, we hope this won't just function as a guide book but also prove to be an enjoyable and inspiring read while you are sitting by the fireside or in the bath on a cold winter's night, dreaming about summer swimming adventures. Cornwall is a land that has inspired countless shanty singers and writers, artists and film makers. And it has inspired us to write this, our love letter to Cornwall.

See you in the water, dreckly!

RIGHTS AND RESPONSIBILITIES

*T*he impact of walkers and swimmers on wild places has become a rather heated issue in recent times. Sadly, some people want to blame us for increased littering in beauty spots, or claim that we have a negative effect on delicate ecosystems. It's true that certain places have become very popular in recent years, and we all need to be aware of our potential impact on the environment. With this in mind we've created a wild swimmers' code, not because these accusations are true, but to show that we are some of the most environmentally aware people enjoying these beauty spots. It's common sense to all of us, but if we leave no trace and take away more litter than we came with, these accusations can no longer be aimed at us. We've also only included walks and swims that are accessible from public footpaths and land: while we are real advocates for access to swim spots and walking routes, we don't want to escalate any existing tensions.

THE WILD SWIMMING CODE

- Car share whenever possible and park sensibly to avoid blocking roads, turning places or gateways.
- Do not leave litter, and pick up any rubbish that you find.
- Do nothing to damage the environment, and take all your rubbish away.
- Do not light fires, including disposable barbecues.
- Respect other water users, including anglers and canoeists/kayakers.
- Leave only footprints, take only memories.

PRACTICALITIES

*T*he Ordnance Survey 1:25,000 Explorer maps are essential. There is the traditional orange folded OS map, and the very handy book form A-Z Adventure Series South West Coast Path, which covers the coastline. The Ordnance Survey is also available as an app, and you can view OS mapping for free on a desktop computer at home (although not on mobile phones or tablets), using Bing Maps. You can print these, and some people take screen grabs of the appropriate section and save them for use later on their phones. You can also buy OS maps for your phone from within a range of apps such as MemoryMap and Viewranger. We give detailed directions for all the walks and swims, doing our best to describe the route, but it's important to realise that you cannot rely on written directions alone, particularly for some of the more remote swims and walks. A map is vital, and a compass is also very useful.

Glynn Valley Works Quarry, Cardinham Moor

WILD SWIMMING SAFETY

Plan your walk, taking necessary supplies and protection; don't forget water, map, compass and waterproofs.

Remember that cold water can limit your swimming endurance. If it is your first outdoor swim of the season, be careful to enter the water slowly and acclimatise. Stay close to the shore until you are comfortable. Wear a wetsuit for added warmth and buoyancy. Do not overestimate your ability. Remember that cold water quickly causes hypothermia – shivering is the first stage.

Don't enter water without first establishing an exit point, especially in fast flowing water. Never jump or dive into water without first checking the depth and whether there are any obstructions. Even if you have jumped/dived there before, always check every time: large obstructions like tree branches and rocks move about underwater, and an area that was previously clear may well be blocked.

Swim in a group wherever possible, or if swimming alone, let people know your movements and take special care.

Take extra care following heavy rainfall, when rivers might be in spate and flowing much faster than normal.

If swimming in the sea, always check the tide before you set out. Watch out in high surf; rip currents can form which take you out to sea, to behind the breaking waves. Swim perpendicular to the pull, not against it, to escape, then body surf back in.

Beware of tidal currents, especially near estuary mouths and around headlands, at mid-tide, and on fortnightly spring tides, when flows are strongest.

If you are concerned about water quality, cover cuts and open wounds with plasters.

TIDES AND WEATHER CONDITIONS FOR CORNWALL

When planning a swim on the coast, it's very useful to look at the wind forecast as well as the tides. If you want calm water, you need to know which way the wind is coming from. The prevailing winds in Cornwall are south-westerly, and if this is the case, then choose a swim spot that faces east. Conversely, if the winds are easterly, then it's a good idea to pick a west- or south-west-facing beach. The principle here is that you don't want the wind blowing from the sea onto the land, as the sea is more likely to be rough. Tides are of course very important, so before you go, find out whether the tide is going out or coming in. In Cornwall during spring tides (the biggest tides, occurring at the time of the full and new moons), high water will always be at about six in the evening, while low water will always be at about noon.

West Looe River

FURTHER INSPIRATION

Charlestown

$\mathcal{S}$everal websites have been invaluable in compiling this book and we would encourage you to visit them for even more tips and inspiration. The South West Coast Path website (**www.southwestcoastpath.org.uk**) was brilliant for suggested routes and in-depth information. Several of the swim walks take in National Trust properties or managed land and beaches, and its website (**www.nationaltrust.org.uk**) is packed with ideas for great days out. iWalk Cornwall is a great website and app, with 258 detailed circular walks in Cornwall, ranging from 2 to 10 miles (**www.iwalkcornwall.co.uk**). The Visit Cornwall website is another really useful resource, with maps and detailed location guide (**www.visitcornwall.com**).

DEVON AND CORNWALL WILD SWIMMING is an informal gathering of mainly weekend walkers and swimmers and is a great way to join in an adventure, although of course you go at your own risk. The group has a wealth of useful information on its website, and organises meet ups through its Facebook pages:
www.devonandcornwallwildswimming.co.uk
www.facebook.com/groups/cornwallwildswimming

FACEBOOK GROUPS for swimmers in Cornwall are plentiful:
Battery Belles and Buoys in Penzance –
www.facebook.com/groups/837855156263795
Blue Tits, Newquay –
www.facebook.com/groups/2378053335838627
Cornwall OWLS (Open Water Leisure Swimmers) –
www.facebook.com/groups/1656419984634159
Gylly Sea Swimmers –
www.facebook.com/groups/1809968085691463
The Outdoor Swimming Society is a national organisation, but is another great place to find like-minded swimmers, information and organised events –
www.outdoorswimmingsociety.com

ORGANISED SWIM EVENTS IN CORNWALL Annual organised swims are popular in Cornwall, many raising money for charity:
Around St Michael's Mount for the Chestnut Appeal – **www.chestnutappeal.org.uk**
Padstow to Rock swim for the Marie Curie charity – email **padstowswim@mariecurie.org.uk**
Castle to Castle swim in Falmouth for the RNLI – **www.falmouthlifeboat.co.uk**

GUIDED SWIMS are offered by local companies:
The Mad Hatters run various events –
www.madhattersportsevents.co.uk
Cornish Rock Tors – **www.cornishrocktors.com**
Sea Swim Cornwall – **www.seaswimcornwall.co.uk**

23

Walk 1

NORTHCOTT MOUTH AND BUDE CIRCULAR

A cliff-top walk that leads to the sea pools of Bude, before returning along the sands at low tide, pausing to swim wherever takes your fancy.

This walk very much relies on setting off two hours before low tide, so you are able to swim in the sea pools safely and walk along the beach without being cut off. We'd hate for the coastguard to have to rescue anyone floating out at sea, clutching a copy of this book above their head. After leaving the National Trust car park at Northcott Mouth ❶, the walk joins the coast path for some impressive views down onto the beach below. The area below Maer Cliff/Maer Downs has been designated an SSSI for the amazing rock formations you will see.

On the cliffs and foreshore you will be able to spot alternating shales, mudstones and siltstones, with beds of sandstone between them. Geologists refer to this as the Bude Formation, moulded on what were then ocean beds during the Carboniferous period, around 300 million years ago. These layers, or strata, were then compressed by movements during a period known as the Variscan Orogeny, when huge pressure created the dramatic patterns you can see today. It's definitely not advisable to go too close to the edge though, as there has been a significant level of rock fall here in recent years.

'Bude, dude' has become known as a bit of a surfer's paradise, and the town's bodacious beaches will soon come into view. First there's Crooklets Beach ❷, then Middle Beach, then Summerleaze Beach and finally Breakwater Beach in the distance. You should also be able to spot the 'Pepper Pot' tower up on the cliffs beyond, which is where we will be walking to after a couple of refreshing swim stops along the way. The path drops down to pass the colourful beach huts and beach concessions, as well as The 2 Minute Charity Shop, another amazing enterprise from the people behind The 2

Minute Beach Clean initiative. They even hire out retro wooden bodyboards, so people don't have to buy the plastic ones that travel halfway across the world before being abandoned after just one use.

Bude Sea Pool ❸ will soon come into view, and it's definitely worth stopping for an invigorating dip here. It is one of the few tidal lidos left in the country and is unique in that the pool is actually built into the natural environment of the cliffs. It was constructed in the 1930s to provide a safe place to swim with the feeling of being in the sea, but away from the often-wild Atlantic surf. Half of the money was put up by the locally prominent Thynne family, and their generosity helped create what remains Bude's number one tourist attraction. Swimming here definitely feels much more of an adventure than in a traditional swimming pool.

The pool is used by 50,000 people every year, and supported by The Friends of Bude Sea Pool (FoBSP). They were set up when there was threat of closure and possible demolition following the loss of council funding, ran a successful Save our Sea Pool campaign, and today help fund the three weeks of vital maintenance each year. Repairs to the sea walls and the removal of tonnes of sand and stone costs around £50,000 a year, so do consider making a donation when you are there.

The next swimming spot is a fascinating piece of social history. Walk towards the sea and the outcrop at the end of the breakwater. This is Barrel Rock, named after its beacon, a barrel on top of a metal pole that warns ships of the dangerous rock stretching out into the sea. The pole is actually the salvaged propeller shaft of the SS Belem, which was wrecked at Northcott Mouth in 1919. As you climb over the rocks you will discover Tommy's Pit ❹, or more formally Sir Thomas's Pit, a magical pool that was built back in 1895.

The pool was funded by Sir Thomas Dyke Acland, 10th Baronet, whose philanthropic generosity financed several projects in Bude including the 'new' breakwater and the Pepper Pot tower. We will also be walking around a section of the Bude Harbour Canal, in which he was a shareholder. He was obviously very popular, with Tommy's Pit affectionately named after him.

Bude's first bathing pool, the Pit was originally reserved for gentlemen only – women were kept a safe distance away at Maer Ladies Bathing Beach, which is known as Crooklets Beach today. Bathers would pay the attendant tuppence to swim and were fined a further penny if they were caught swimming naked. Hence the limerick:

There once was a young man from Bude
Who fancied a dip in the nude
For a thruppenny bit
He could swim in Tom's Pit
Which included the fine for being rude!

The sea pool can only be found and used at lower tides, as at high tide there is a real risk of being smashed against the rocks or swept out to sea. With this in mind, Sir Thomas's son compiled some of the first ever tide timetables and placed a half-tide marker rock at the end of Coach Rock on Summerleaze Beach. You will also spot numbers on the wall at the sea end of the pool, which once marked the depth; don't take these as accurate today, because sand is being washed in and out all of the time. After doing a few mini-laps, you might want to also have a dip in Breakwater Beach, just off to the left. Although only a matter of metres away from popular Summerleaze Beach, it's usually deserted. Do bear in mind there is no lifeguard cover here, and there can be strong currents.

Continuing your walk across the breakwater you will pass Chapel Rock, where a chapel dedicated to

St Michael once stood. Apparently, it was originally occupied by a hermit who would keep a fire burning at this vantage point to guide mariners to safe haven. There is a staircase to the top, but we are about to walk much higher, up to the Pepper Pot ❺ on Efford Down. It was built in 1835 by Sir Thomas Acland, as part of his series of ambitious development plans. He enlisted Plymouth architect George Wightwick to create the structure, which served the dual purpose of being a refuge for the coastguard and also an ornamental feature of the baronet's Efford Estate.

The Pepper Pot is modelled on the Temple of the Winds in Athens, and the views are outstanding: on a clear day you can see down towards Padstow to your left and Morwenstow and Lundy Island to the north. It stands at what is now known as Compass Point, since each side of the octagonal tower has one of the points of the compass carved in as a frieze. The tower was dismantled and rebuilt further inland around 1900, due to the eroding cliffs, and apparently it is now seven degrees out of alignment, just in case you were checking with your compass against it. There are plans afoot to move it again, due to further erosion, so perhaps this time they can correct the small mistake from the last century.

The walk now takes us back down towards the beach and the Bude Canal ❻ and its unique sea lock. The canal was built in the 1920s to transport lime-rich sea sand inland to be used as manure on farms that suffered from acidic and unproductive soil. It was planned that other cargoes could include coal, slate, iron, bricks and timber, with farm produce also being exported. The canal was never a major success for the shareholders, although it did prove invaluable for the farms it was initially built to support. Trade declined dramatically when the railway reached Bude in 1998, with the canal closing just three years later. The Bude Canal Regeneration Project was set

up in 2006 and restored the first two miles of the waterway up to Helebridge.

We cross the lock to walk along the canal to Lower Wharf. The warehouses that would have supported the workings of the canal have today been transformed into funky eateries and craft shops. Even the canal itself is busy once more, although today the barges have been replaced with rowing boats, swan boats and VW Beetle-style pedalos. Beside the warehouses we pass Bude Castle Heritage Centre ❼. This was the home of Victorian inventor Sir Goldsworthy Gurney, who managed an impressive engineering feat when he built his 'castle' on the shifting sand dunes.

Amongst his many inventions was a method of lighting for his home that used the injection of oxygen into an oil flame. This created an extremely bright light that was then reflected by a series of mirrors. So successful was the invention, known as Bude-Light, that it was used to illuminate Pall Mall, Trafalgar Square and the Houses of Parliament. His experiments with steam also helped power Stephenson's record-breaking rocket, while his other illuminating experiments led to the development of limelight, which was used in theatres and music halls across the globe.

Following the path past the conical Bude Light sculpture, created in 2000 to commemorate Gurney's invention, we turn left to cross Nanny Moore's Bridge ❽, a packhorse bridge that dates back to at least the 18th century. Originally known as Town Bridge, the Grade II listed structure was renamed after Nanny Moore, who lived in one of the Levens Cottages next to it. She was a 'dipper' or bathing machine attendant, providing a valuable service for those women wanting to enter the sea with their modesty intact. Why a bridge was named after her seems lost in the sands of time, although we may assume it was because she was either lovely and highly respected, or a tyrant.

We would like to think it was the former. The bridge is a prime spot to watch the annual duck race that takes place on Lifeboat Day over the August Bank Holiday weekend.

The walk follows Summerleaze Crescent and then drops back down onto the beach and below the seawater pool, to make your way below the cliffs back towards Northcott Mouth. It's a lovely walk at low tide, with the dramatically eroding cliffs towering above you on one side, and the roaring Atlantic Ocean on the other. The seemingly endless sand (the tidal range is 7 metres) is broken up by the rocky fingers of the Bude Formation. These upended strata provide plenty of rockpools to explore and places to hang your clothes before a dip. The water colour here is extraordinary, and it's a great place to play in the surf before continuing the walk back to Northcott Mouth. This beach is owned by the National Trust and marks the start of an Area of Outstanding Natural Beauty that continues right up to the Devon border.

If you have time, it's worth exploring the northern end of Northcott Mouth near Manachurch Point, to see if the wreck of the SS Belem is visible in the sand. The steamship ran aground in 1917, although thankfully all 33 men were safely rescued. The remains include the propeller shaft – a section of which was used for the beacon at Barrel Rock, next to Tommy's Pit – and the boilers.

It's then just a short walk back up to the car park, although we would highly recommend a stop at the Rustic Tea Gardens for a cream tea. Open between March and October, the tea garden has been run by Margaret Frost (and her mother Louise before her) since 1963. Many people make the bold claim that it's the best Cornish cream tea in the county and we would probably have to agree. Just remember, its jam first and then the cream. Obviously.

DIRECTIONS

1 Leave the car park and turn left onto the track. Go through the gate onto the coast path, with the sea on your right. Keep following it.
0.9 miles

2 You reach Crooklets Beach, where you can stop for a swim if you like. Stay on the coast path, around the rear of the beach, past the beach huts and concessions.
0.2 miles

3 Bude Sea Pool on your right is another potential swim stop. After your swim, head onto the beach and bear left towards a mast with a barrel on top and the causeway.
0.2 miles

4 Tommy's Pit is near the mast. Take a dip in the seawater pool and perhaps the little beach to the south. From the little beach, walk back to the causeway and turn right along it in the direction of the tower on the hillside. When you reach the end of the causeway, turn right to follow the coast path up.
0.3 miles

5 From the Pepper Pot, follow the path down to the right-hand side of the main beach and descend the steps onto the road. Follow the road about 150 metres then cross the lock gates.
0.2 miles

6 With the canal on your right, follow it inland towards the converted warehouses ahead. Bear left through the Wharf car park and walk along the road.
0.3 miles

7 You can divert off left to the Bude Castle Heritage Centre. Head back to the road and pass the conical fountain with flower beds on your left.
0.2 miles

8 Cross Nanny Moore's bridge, turn left along the road, then drop down onto the beach and walk to the left of the sea pool. Walk along the beach all the way back to Northcott Mouth, stopping for swims wherever takes your fancy. Follow the path in front of the Bude

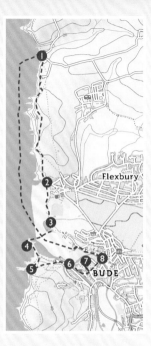

Castle Heritage Centre on your left and then the conical sculpture on your right. Turn left at the road and follow it to the footbridge.
1.8 miles

29

Walk 2

ST NECTAN'S GLEN AND BOSSINEY HAVEN CIRCULAR

A spectacular walk of great contrasts, taking in an ancient place of pilgrimage, a dramatic rocky gorge and a beach complete with natural arch. We swim in both fresh and salt water.

INFORMATION

DISTANCE: 3.5 miles
TIME: Allow 6 hours
MAP: OS Explorer OL111 Bude, Boscastle and Tintagel
START POINT: Parking area in Bossiney village at top of path down to Bossiney Haven (SX 067 889, PL34 0AY); in summer months a field is also open for parking here, £1.
END POINT: Parking area in Bossiney village.
PUBLIC TRANSPORT: Bus route 95 between Bude and Camelford stops in Bossiney.
SWIMMING: Rocky Valley (SX 072 896), Bossiney Haven (SX 066 894).
PLACES OF INTEREST: St Nectan's Glen, Rocky Valley, the steel footbridge at Tintagel.
REFRESHMENTS: St Nectan's Café is on the walk route, and has huge windows opening out onto a terrace (01840 779538, PL34 0HL). The Bossiney Tea Rooms is in a Victorian property just by the car park, with a lovely garden and conservatory where you can eat outside in the summer months (01840 779327, PL34 0AY).
EASIER ACCESS: It's just 0.3 miles from the car park downhill to Bossiney Haven. You can drive into St Nectan's Glen if you have a 4x4 but phone ahead first, and there are numerous steps down to the waterfall.
NEARBY SWIM SPOTS: Trebarwith Strand is stunning, with the remains of an old harbour at the southern end; Port Gaverne is a u-shaped cove which is like a long swimming pool at high water.

The walk starts in the village of Bossiney ❶ just along from Tintagel where a stunning steel footbridge – dubbed the Gossamer Gateway to Avalon by *The Guardian* – opened in 2019. This whole area feels a bit mystical, with its Arthurian legends and St Nectan's Glen, which is a place of pilgrimage for both pagans and Christians. You'll understand why when you see the hauntingly beautiful and frankly extraordinary natural scenery on this walk, which makes one feel quite insignificant in the greater scheme of things.

This walk is best done when the winds are east or south-easterly, as the swim spot at Bossiney Haven is usually calm then. It is also sheltered from the prevailing south westerlies, but if you visit when there are northerly winds, you may encounter a lot of surf and swell. It is also good to plan your walk to arrive at Bossiney Haven around a couple of hours either side of high tide.

Although the walk is short in miles, allow plenty of time, as there is so much to see that you can quite happily spend a whole day completing it. You'll visit St Nectan's Glen en route, which takes at least an hour, and you can while away a lot of time in Rocky Valley, which makes a perfect picnic stop.

After a pleasant walk through fields, you enter the woods of St Nectan's Glen ❹. On a sunny day it is absolutely magical here, with shafts of light bursting through the trees, and lots of dappled shade. The River Trevillet gurgles by, and soon you'll cross a small footbridge where you will see an enormous log, studded with thousands of coins. It looks rather like an armadillo or hedgehog; this is a money tree where people leave offerings to the spirits of the glen in the hope that it will bring them luck.

The Victorian novelist Wilkie Collins visited St Nectan's Glen as part of a hike around Cornwall in 1850, and wrote about it in his book *Rambles Beyond Railways*. It seems that back then, the path through the woods was not such easy going. He noted: "It seems as if all the foliage which ought to have grown on the Cornish moorlands, had been mischievously crammed into this place, within the narrow limits of one Cornish valley… Tangled branches and thorny bushes press against you in front and behind, meet over your head, knock off your cap, and tear your coat skirts… they seem possessed with a living power of opposition, and commissioned by some evil genius of Fairy Mythology to prevent mortal footsteps from intruding into the valley."

Some say the 6th century St Nectan lived at the top of the waterfall and would ring a silver bell in stormy weather to warn sailors of impending danger. Others of a more pagan persuasion say St Nectan was never here, and the name is a corruption of that of a Celtic water spirit, Nechtan. Early maps spurn both, naming it Nathan's Cave (a corruption of 'cuva', the Cornish for tub). Whatever the true history behind the name, which we will never know, the place draws visitors from all over the world, keen to experience its mystical power.

The path takes you to a gate where you enter and pay to view the waterfall. You follow a walkway to view it from the top and halfway down. It is absolutely stunning. The water gushes from a high hole in the rock before thundering through another round hole, like a moon gate, and crashing into the small pool below. Although you can't swim there, it's well worth getting into your costume and going under the waterfall for the most invigorating massage. People leave ribbons and mementos around the waterfall for luck, but it doesn't feel tacky. If you need refreshment, there is a very good café on site.

After visiting the waterfall, head back through the woods and onto the lane, turning downhill and crossing the main coast road to pick up the footpath into Rocky Valley ❼. You'll see the ruins of an old mine, where there are two small, rather odd carvings of round mazes on the valley wall. There is a plaque from the 1950s which says they date from the Bronze Age, but more recent opinion has suggested they are no more than a few hundred years old. Our guess is that they might have been made by some Victorian entrepreneur, who was keen to attract tourists to the area.

As you walk through Rocky Valley be prepared for a surprise. You twist through a narrow gorge of grey slate, like a miniature version of the Grand Canyon, turn a corner, and there is the sea, an enticing patch of blue at the end. This stunning scenery was created by the river running along a fault line in the slate millions of years ago. The water flows through a beautiful sequence of waterfalls, cauldrons and pools. The immediate temptation is to swim down through them and out to the sea at the end; needless to say, this is extremely dangerous – please do not even think about doing it! However, it is huge fun to wallow in the pools and enjoy the waterfalls. It's a great spot to stop for lunch, and on wild days the sea crashing into the gorge is a dramatic sight.

This is the kind of place that can vary enormously according to what time of year you visit it. In dry periods it is a benign spot, where you can spend a few hours sunbathing on the rocky ledges and dipping in the pools. But in winter it is a different story. The writer Daphne du Maurier had this to say in her book *Vanishing Cornwall*: "The narrowness of the gorge impels the water, swollen with winter rains, to course the faster, and white with foam it twists and tumbles over its stony bed to a sudden flat surface where, smooth for an instant, it plunges from the canyon to the open sea." She went on to ponder the special atmosphere of the valley: "The place has the impersonality of somewhere superbly dissociated from humankind, even from life itself. There are no gulls perching upon the ledges or the clefts, no sheep grazing on the headlands beyond. The force of matter is pre-eminent, hard rock challenging the elemental thrust of water."

After Rocky Valley, there's a steep climb up to the headland at the top. The views are absolutely breathtaking. You walk along the top of the cliffs, passing through Bossiney Common, and then follow the path down to Bossiney Haven ⓫. From the cliffs there is a good view of Elephant Rock ahead, which has a tall, slim natural arch within it. It does look very much like an elephant, the arch forming the space between the elephant's forequarters and its trunk, and you can swim through it around two hours either side of high tide.

Bossiney Cove is very much a low-tide beach, but if you want the best swimming conditions rather than beach, visit it at high tide. You have not only the fun of swimming under the elephant's trunk, but an enormous cave to the left beyond it where the waves echo dramatically. Bossiney Haven is recessed right at the back of the cove, as sheltered and safe as its name suggests. On a calm day you can explore all its caves, inlets and gullies either by swimming or, if the tide is low, by walking. Lye Rock, to the left of the beach, was once home to Cornwall's only colony of puffins.

The walk back up to the car park is steep but short. It's thought that medieval farmers would bring seaweed up from the beach to use as fertiliser on their crops; there are the remains of ancient farming systems at Bossiney Common on the top of the cliffs. Opposite the parking is the Bossiney Tea Rooms, established in 2019, and there is also a rather good ice cream van in the car park during the summer months.

❸ Turn left along the road and then after a very short distance climb a stile on the right where there is a granite sign saying 'Little Clifden 2018'. Walk through the field to the edge of the woods.
0.1 miles

❹ Take the path downhill through the woods, cross a bridge and keep following the path with the river on your right until you reach St Nectan's Glen.
0.5 miles

❶ From the car park walk south-west along the road for a very short distance and then turn left opposite Ocean Cove holiday park and where there is a 'public footpath' sign through Bossiney Bay Holiday Village.
0.1 miles

❺ After visiting the waterfall retrace your steps through the woods and back to the road. Turn right.
0.7 miles

❷ Walk through the holiday lodges, then follow the sign for 'Halgabron and Waterfall', cross a stream and head through the fields to a small road.
0.4 miles

❻ At the farm, keep walking down the road until you reach the larger coast road.
0.2 miles

❼ Cross the coast road and follow the path downhill by Trevillett Mill Holiday Cottages, bearing right and crossing the bridge over the river.
0.3 miles

❽ You will reach a ruined mill where you can see the labyrinth carvings. Cross a footbridge over the river and follow the path down to Rocky Valley.
0.1 miles

❾ Pause at the end of Rocky Valley to take in the views and swim. Then continue on the coast path with a steep climb up to the headland.
0.1 miles

❿ From the headland, follow the coast path along the cliffs and down to Bossiney Haven.
0.4 miles

⓫ From Bossiney Haven, retrace the path up from the beach and carry straight on up to the car park.
0.2 miles

Walk 3

PENTIRE, LUNDY HOLE AND PORT QUIN CIRCULAR

A dazzling and dramatic walk around huge headlands with vast views, peppered with secret coves crammed with caves and a village with a poignant past.

INFORMATION

DISTANCE: 9 miles (shorter routes of 3 and 5.5 miles are detailed on p40)
TIME: Allow all day
MAP: OS Explorer 106 Newquay and Padstow
START POINT: Lead Mines National Trust car park at Pentireglaze SW 940 799 PL27 6UA.
END POINT: Lead Mines National Trust car park.
PUBLIC TRANSPORT: Bus route 10 from Launceston to Wadebridge stops in Polzeath, from where you could start the walk at point 3.
SWIMMING: Pentireglaze Haven (SW 933 796), reef pools (SW 929 799), unnamed cove, low tide beach (SW 937 806), Lundy Bay (SW 958 799), Port Quin inlet (SW 970 806).
PLACES OF INTEREST: The Rumps promontory fort, Doyden Castle.
REFRESHMENTS: Nothing on route, bring supplies. The Galleon Beach Café in Polzeath makes wood-fired pizzas on the beach (01208 869643, PL27 6TB). The Cracking Crab on the clifftop in Polzeath specialises in seafood (01208 862333, PL27 6TD).
EASIER ACCESS: Port Quin is easily accessible from the road, and a small car park is close to the beach - high tide access only. Polzeath main beach has a car park on it; except at high water there's a long walk over the sand.
NEARBY SWIM SPOTS: Daymer Bay is popular with swimmers, with regular local meet-ups (search for Cornwall Open Water Leisure Swimmers) on Facebook. Port Isaac and Port Gaverne are sheltered.

This is a beautiful and strenuous walk along one of the most dramatic stretches of the north Cornish coast. If you don't want to do the full distance, there are several shorter options described in the directions. The particularly wonderful thing about this walk is the views. Most of the time you are on the cliffs, walking above the sea. The first few beaches are all best at low water, while the last, Port Quin, is best at high, so we suggest starting the walk at low tide; by the time you get to Port Quin, you should have enough water to swim in.

The walk starts in an area called Pentireglaze, where there used to be a lead and silver mine that operated for around 300 years between Tudor and Victorian times. It became unprofitable and closed in the 1850s, although the engine house stood another 100 years until it was demolished in 1957. The car park where we start the walk is on the site of the old engine house.

The walk takes you along to Pentire Farm ❷, a handsome stone building that can be rented for holidays. This whole area is owned by the National Trust, which is gradually creating new permissive paths, helping walkers to avoid the roads. You then head down a little valley to the first beach, Pentireglaze Haven ❸, fondly known by locals and regular holidaymakers alike as 'Baby Bay'. Not far from here is the legendary Robbie Love's campsite, established in the rave era of the late 1980s. Forty years later, it is still going strong, and provides cheap accommodation for the many seasonal workers who come to work in Polzeath for the summer, as well as for surfers and walkers.

Baby Bay is an inlet next to the main beach at Polzeath; at low tide you can walk between the two but at high it is cut off. It's a lovely spot away from the crowds. Moving on, the walk takes you up and around the beautiful Pentire headland. There is an extensive reef on the southern side, where there are stunning gullies and rockpools to explore at mid- to low tide, as well as a tiny shingle beach. There are steps off the path ❹ where you can get down. The walk continues along to Pentire Point ❺, from where there are extensive views back along the Camel Estuary and over to Stepper Point on the other side, with the daymark navigation tower on top, looking like a mine chimney. You will also spot Newlands Island to the north-west, where many seabirds, including kittiwakes, cormorants and shags, make their home. From here you head north-east to the Rumps ❻, a double headland jutting out into the sea. Along the way you pass a plaque commemorating Laurence Binyon's composition on these cliffs of the poem 'For the Fallen', which includes the famous "They shall grow not old, as we that are left grow old" lines, used in memorial services around the world.

It is worth crossing the small isthmus onto the Rumps from Pentire Head to have a look around. In the 2nd century BC, Iron Age people established a fort here, which would have been protected by a wooden palisade on ditches and ramparts across the isthmus to defend their home from the landward side. The site was excavated between 1963 and 1967, and the remains of several roundhouses were found, as well as pottery, weaving materials and amphora fragments, which suggest the occupants traded with the Mediterranean.

As you leave the Rumps and carry on along the coast, you will see another islet, small and conical, which is called the Mouls. Puffins breed here, and the best way to see them is by taking a boat trip from Padstow. The birds are migrants, returning to

Cornwall to breed in March or April. They make burrows in which they lay their eggs, and the chicks – called pufflings – hatch in May and June.

The next swim stop is found by following a tiny path off the main coast path ❼ below Pentire Farm to an unnamed, hidden cove ❽. Be warned, the final descent to the beach is extremely challenging, involving a climb down a pretty sheer rock face: do not attempt it unless you are a competent and fit scrambler. However, if you can make it down, it is perfect, with views across to the Mouls, fine sand, a large cave and a pretty gully. Just be aware that the beach disappears at high tide. If all you want to do is swim, then high tide might be the best time to go, because you can just swim off the rocks, rather than have the treacherous climb down to the beach.

After climbing back up to the coast path, you head left and continue, with more stunning views as you go. After passing Downhedge Cove ⓭ the coast path continues through a field, and at the beginning of the next field, you will notice a well-worn, narrow path off to the left heading towards the edge of the cliff. This leads down to Carnweather Point, a popular fishing spot which is not for the faint-hearted, with a rope to help you climb down. It would probably be fun to swim off the rocks there too, although we did not try it!

Shortly after, you reach Lundy Hole, a collapsed sea cave that you pass on the left. A large oval shaft in the cliffs, it fills with water at high tide. According to legend, St Minver was minding her own business, sitting on a rock combing her hair, when the Devil came along. She threw her comb at him, and he was so taken aback he created Lundy Hole into which he fled. Although it sounds somewhat implausible, it might be worth carrying a comb just in case.

Just after Lundy Hole is a descent to Lundy Bay **⑩**, which at low tide joins Epphaven Cove next door. Both are stunning, with lots of interesting rockpools and gullies to explore. Just remember not to fall asleep when the tide is coming in, as both beaches disappear, and you may find yourself getting washed away!

After a dip, you carry on along the coast path to reach Doyden Castle **⑪**, a tiny but distinctive Gothic building on the headland looking out to sea. More of a folly than a castle, it was built by Samuel Symons in around 1840 as a place to entertain his friends – rather like a glorified beach hut for people with money. Apparently, it was a bit of a den of iniquity back in the day, with riotous drinking and gambling. Now it's a National Trust holiday let, one of their most popular – less riotous, but there's no reason why you shouldn't indulge in a bit of gambling and drinking if you're lucky enough to go and stay there.

The next and final swim spot is in Port Quin **⑫**, a blissful U-shaped bay that fills up like a swimming pool at high tide. If the tide is still low, it's best to stop before you get to the village, at an inlet just after Doyden Castle, as you can swim off the rocks here. The village itself is tiny, with a slipway bearing the legend 'Property of P.A. Vernon' impressed into the concrete. On a summer's day it is the picture of calm, but in winter fierce storms can race up the bay. There is a sad side to this place, which is known locally as the 'village that died'. Local legend has it that in the 19th century all the village's fishermen were wiped out in a storm, leaving 32 widows who eventually left to find new lives elsewhere. Today the remaining cottages are all National Trust holiday lets and the only trade is tourism; it's very popular with kayakers and paddleboarders, as well as us wild swimmers.

SHORTER OPTIONS

Pentire Head: Follow points 1–8, then after coming up from the hidden cove, turn left onto the coast path but then very soon take the right-hand fork back up to Pentire Farm and retrace your steps back to the car park. **3 miles**

Pentire Head and Lundy Bay: Follow points 1–10, then turn back on the coast path to point 13 and follow instructions from there to get back to car park. **5.5 miles**

Lundy Bay and Port Quin: This is easiest done as an out-and-back walk, as the only circular route involves walking on roads. Park at the National Trust car park for Lundy Bay at SW 952 795. Follow the signed path opposite down to Lundy Bay, joining the coast path just west of Lundy Hole, and follow steps 10–12 to Port Quin, then retrace your steps to get back. **4 miles**

DIRECTIONS

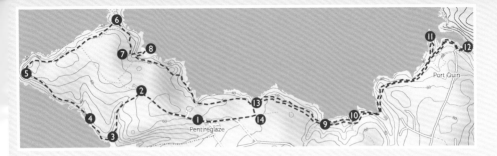

1 Walking out of the car park, face towards Polzeath and turn right along the road towards Pentire Farm. Follow the road through a wooden pedestrian gate beside a five-bar gate, over the cattle grid.
0.3 miles

2 At Pentire Farm, take the footpath to the left opposite the farmhouse, signed Coast Path and Pentire Haven.
0.3 miles

3 You reach the coast at Pentireglaze, and the first swim spot. Turn right by the wooden sign saying Pentire Head and keep following the coast path.
0.3 miles

4 Shortly after you go through a gate, you will see some little steps down to the rocks on the left. This is a lovely place to find pools in the lower half of the tide, when a little cove here is also accessible.
0.5 miles

5 Keep following the path along the edge of the cliffs until you reach Pentire Point. Look back for great views of the Camel Estuary before continuing along the footpath.
0.8 miles

6 The coast path turns at the Rumps. You can divert here to explore if you wish, then head back to continue along the coast path.
0.3 miles

7 Look for a small rough path off to the left, which leads down to an unnamed, hidden cove; it is just before a fork in the path where a wooden sign points to Pentire Farm. Follow the path down and climb through the wooden bars and then down onto the rocks to reach the cove, retracing your steps to the coast path after. This is a challenging climb down rocks and only suitable for confident climbers. Do not attempt it with small children.
0.1 miles

8 From the cove, head back to the coast path and turn left. Keep following it with the sea on your left.
1.5 miles

9 You reach a fork with a wooden post with a yellow acorn. Keep left here, passing Lundy Hole on your left, follow the path on to a wooden staircase on your left; the final descent to Lundy Bay also involves some scrambling down over rocks.
0.2 miles

10 From Lundy Bay, retrace your steps and turn left along the coast path, keeping the sea on your left again.
0.8 miles

11 You will see Doyden Castle to your left. After diverting along the road for a look around, rejoin the coast path, which then joins the lane down to Port Quin.
0.4 miles

12 After a dip at Port Quin, retrace your steps back along the coast path, passing Lundy Bay on your right, as far as Downhedge Cove.
1.8 miles

13 Turn left off the coast path through a gap in the stone wall above Downhedge Cove, by an impressive cleft in the cliffs, following the sign for Pentireglaze. Walk along the left-hand edge of the field.
0.1 miles

14 At the end of the field, turn right following the wooden Pentireglaze sign and take the track back to the road and on to the car park.
0.5 miles

41

Walk 4

CARDINHAM MOOR LAKES CIRCULAR

This spectacular walk over a little-visited part of Bodmin Moor takes in two beautiful lakes, a stone row, and one of Cornwall's best-preserved Iron Age forts. You need clear weather, and a compass would not go amiss, as the paths are not well defined.

INFORMATION

DISTANCE: 6 miles
TIME: Allow 5-6 hours
MAP: OS Explorer 109 Bodmin
START POINT: Bellamin's Tor car park on A30 (SX 132 725, PL30 4HP); look out for brown Temple Fishery sign.
END POINT: Bellamin's Tor car park.
PUBLIC TRANSPORT: None
SWIMMING: Burnt Heath Pool (SX 128 721), Glynn Valley Pool (SX 142 718).
PLACES OF INTEREST: Colvannick Stone Row, Bury Castle, Glynn Valley Works.
REFRESHMENTS: Nothing on the walk itself, so take supplies. The Jamaica Inn nearby is world famous, after Daphne du Maurier wrote a novel set there, and it also has a small museum about her (01566 86250, PL15 7TS). Woods Café is a charming eaterie in the middle of nearby Cardinham Woods with home-made food (01208 78111, PL30 4AL).
EASIER ACCESS: It is a flat walk of about 0.4 miles to the first swim spot from the car park. The second swim spot at Glynn Valley is unfortunately a longer walk into the moor, although you could drive up the no-through road to Maidenwell, from where it is 0.5 miles walk along a flat track.
NEARBY SWIM SPOTS: There is a beautiful high tide swim in the Fowey estuary at St Winnow near Lerryn; Trebarwith Strand on the north coast is a lovely beach with caves and rock pools.

T he walk starts in the somewhat inauspicious surroundings of a car park on the busy A30, but never fear, you will soon be away from the thunder of traffic and into another world of moorland wilderness. Here you will discover many fascinating relics, from thousands of years ago right up to the recent past. The walk skirts a firing range called Millpool: if there is firing, a red flag will be flying, but the walk route stays outside the range, so you will be fine if you stick to it. You can check firing times in advance at: www.gov.uk/government/publications/millpool-firing-times.

Very soon after you set off you come to the first swim spot, an old china clay pit ❷, which used to be the Burnt Heath China Clay Works. It is now a large pond with a lovely shelving entrance, but really deep in the middle. In the summer there are beautiful blue dragonflies around the edges, and you may share the pool with ponies who like to come and drink there. Swimming as the traffic goes by on the horizon is a slightly surreal experience, but rather fun too, feeling smug as you enjoy the water while everyone else is stuck in their cars. It's also a good place to remember for future visits when you might be travelling down the A30 and desperately need a quick dip!

After your swim, you head south and into the wilder landscape of Cardinham Moor, towards St Bellarmin's Tor, which has a prominent trig point on the top. En route to the tor, you will come across a very large stone leaning on its side ❸. This is in fact the terminal stone of the Colvannick Stone Row, which was only discovered relatively

recently by the Ordnance Survey during a field investigation in 1973. It first appeared on the OS map in 1984, but many enthusiasts found it difficult to locate. In 2004 Mark Camp, a keen walker and historian who lives locally, found it by accident. At the time he wrote: "To be honest I wasn't looking for a stone row... I was just out for a walk after visiting the remains of the nearby clay works. And I was lost... well not exactly, but I had given up on finding the footpath and was just heading west into the sun hoping to find a wall somewhere... Next thing I know there is this huge great stone leaning at some precarious angle in front of me. Could this be the stone row that should be further to the north? Well, yes it was."

The stones are much bigger than those of most stone rows that are found in Cornwall, and when they were all standing they would have been an imposing sight. Some have now fallen, but those that remain are still pretty impressive. No one knows why our Bronze Age ancestors created these rows, but there can be no doubt they had some significance.

You continue on with the firing range on your left to St Bellarmin's Tor ❸, from where there are amazing views southwards down to the sea at Fowey; the 'Cornish Alps' of the china clay workings around St Austell are also visible in the same direction. To the north, you can see the highest point on Bodmin,

Brown Willy, and next to it Rough Tor. As you head down from the tor, look out for the remains of the medieval St Bellarmin's Chapel, which is very well hidden in the litter strewn around the sides of the tor. It is difficult to spot among the stones, and there is some dispute as to whether it was actually a chapel at all – some believe it was just a pen for stock.

After descending from the tor, you cross some marshy land (skirt around it if wet) and then head uphill through an area studded with gorse and small hawthorn trees. You emerge and walk towards the southern end of the firing range. As you walk along you may notice a sweet smell; there is a camomile lawn underfoot, which is very unusual in moorland like this. There are more amazing views as you round the end of the range, including down to Cardinham church. It was damaged by German bombs intended for Bodmin during the Second World War, although you wouldn't know that to look at it today.

You continue along to Bury Castle ❾, one of the best-preserved Iron Age forts in Cornwall. It is vast and almost circular, and makes a great place to stop for lunch. The ramparts are clearly visible, and although much of the ancient monument has been lost, you certainly get a strong sense of the extent and grandeur of this fort, which would have been created by a tribal chieftain about 2,000 years ago.

From the fort, the walk continues down a pretty path between fields and then along a lane past granite houses before emerging back on the moor. You follow a field boundary to a track, which takes you towards the unmistakable twin peaks of the old Glynn Valley China Clay Works ahead. Before you reach them, look out for the fallen chimney of the workings on the right (just before ❿) – marked on the OS map. This is something of an oddity, which is fun to crawl through. It is a strange feeling, seeing the soot from years ago still clinging to the inside of the chimney; it's just about the only chance you'll ever get to be inside a chimney!

You then arrive at the spectacular remains of the old china clay works, a huge lake overlooked by the dramatic conical spoil tips from the old workings. This was one of about 20 china clay pits on Bodmin Moor, which was a very busy place in Cornwall in the 19th and early 20th centuries. According to Historic England, the works opened in 1875, and were in operation on and off until the middle of the 20th century.

The lake is an absolutely awesome place to swim. There is a shipping container by the water which is an off-grid holiday let, so it is best to walk around to the northern part of the lake and get in there ❶ so as not to disturb any residents. Saying that, this whole area is open access land, which means that everyone has the right to walk here.

You plunge into the soft, silky waters of the lake and can swim for ages before having to turn around. At some times of the year the water is incredibly clear, with beautiful green and copper-coloured weeds that sparkle underwater in the light. In the summer it can get very warm, and swallows and swifts swoop around you as you swim; it is magical. In winter it is a total contrast: dark, dramatic and cold, still magical but in a different way.

After your swim, you continue to the north, and then bear left along a stream and uphill again, following the red and white posts of the firing range, which will guide you back up towards the car park. It's then back into the warmth of your car and onto the A30 to rejoin the rat race, but with a smile upon your face as you remember these hidden secret swim spots that most of the other drivers will never get to experience.

DIRECTIONS

❶ Leave the car park by the gate at the cattle grid end and then turn right, walking back along the fence on your right and then towards the pool already visible ahead.
0.4 miles

❷ After your dip, follow the rough path to the south of the pool, heading for St Bellarmin's Tor, which you will see in the distance. You cross a faint track and keep straight on.
0.2 miles

❸ At a large stone where ponies often scratch themselves, you can look back over your right shoulder to see the stone row, and divert to explore the alignment. Then return to the large stone and continue due south to St Bellarmin's Tor.
0.5 miles

❹ From St Bellarmin's Tor, continue walking south, aiming for the gorse-covered uphill slope ahead. You will see the red-and-white posts marking the firing area; always keep to the

right of these. Cross a marshy patch (you may need to walk around if very wet) to reach the gorse area.
0.2 miles

❺ Follow the path through the gorse to emerge onto a more open area.
0.3 miles

❻ Bear left across the open ground, keeping the fence on your left, until you come to a tarmacked track across your path.
0.2 miles

7 Turn left and follow the track to the signed entrance to Millpool Range. Turn right onto a rougher track here and very shortly (about 50 metres on) you see a public footpath sign where you can go straight on or turn right. Head right, and follow the field boundary on your left.
0.3 miles

8 At the end of the boundary is a metal gate. Turn left through here to another metal gate and a stile. Cross the stile and head over the field bearing right to the opposite corner, where you go through to the next field.
0.2 miles

9 On your right in this field is Bury Castle. Divert here for a look at the views and maybe a bite to eat. Then head back out of the castle at its northern edge and turn right, continuing on the path across the field to a stile.
0.1 miles

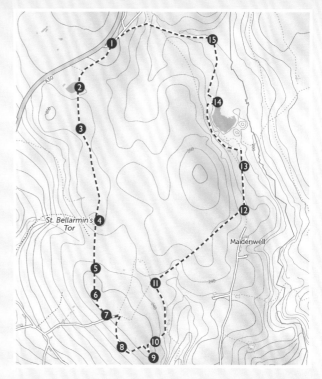

10 Cross the stile and walk down the path between the fields until it reaches a track. Turn left here and walk past several old stone houses. Ignore gateways to right and left and keep going on the path, which becomes narrow between the hedges.
0.4 miles

11 You reach a five-bar metal gate, which is the entrance back onto the moor. Go through and turn right at a wooden post with a blue and a yellow arrow, walking alongside the wall on your right. You will see a big clump of conifer trees ahead; pass these on your right and then start to head downhill, looking across to

your left where you will see the distinctive alp-like spoil heaps.
0.7 miles

12 You meet a gravel track. Turn left along it, and look out for the fallen chimney on your right as you go, for a diversion to crawl inside it.
0.2 miles

13 Where the track forks, bear right towards the spoil heaps. Follow the path as it bears to the left around the back of the shipping container house, and walk around the lake until you get to the north-west corner for a secluded swim.
0.6 miles

14 After your swim, head back to the path and follow the red-and-white posts, keeping them on your left. You can follow the posts all the way back to the car park, although at first they are leading away from it – if there is no firing, there is a path to the left of the posts that cuts off two sides of the triangle.
0.5 miles

15 You reach a stream where the posts turn left at the corner of the range. Walk alongside the stream, with the poles on your left, up the hill and back to the car park.
0.6 miles

Walk 5

LITTLE PETHERICK CREEK CIRCULAR

A magnificent walk through the fascinating and ever-changing environment of the Camel Estuary and one of its major creeks, with amazing views down the river to the sea, and up to Bodmin Moor.

INFORMATION

DISTANCE: 6.5 miles
TIME: 6 hours
MAP: OS Explorer 106 Newquay and Padstow
START POINT: Car park at Old Town, near Padstow (SW 939 738, PL27 7QL).
END POINT: Car park at Old Town.
PUBLIC TRANSPORT: None to the car park, but Padstow is served by bus routes 11A from Bodmin Parkway, 56 and A5 from Newquay and 219 from Truro. From Padstow you could walk out to Dennis Cove, and start there.
SWIMMING: Oldtown Cove (SW 938 740), Little Petherick Creek Bridge (SW 923 741), Dennis Cove (SW 921 744).
PLACES OF INTEREST: Little Petherick Church, Dennis Hill Obelisk, Sea Mills.
REFRESHMENTS: None en route (the Old Mill Bistro in Little Petherick is only open in the evenings). The Pickwick Inn in nearby Burgois has a beautiful dining room (01841 540361, PL27 7QQ). Padstow is stuffed with eateries, including several of chef Rick Stein's establishments from the very posh to the more casual; they prefer you to book online, but you can also phone (0841 532700, PL28 8AP, rickstein.com).
EASIER ACCESS: The first swim spot on the Camel is close to the car park (5 mins walk); steps lead up to the Camel Trail but then it is a short walk along the flat Camel Trail to the beach. Little Petherick Creek is a further 10 minutes walk along the Camel Trail; there is a small descent down a path to get to it.
NEARBY SWIM SPOTS: Trevone Bay west of Padstow has a beautiful beach and a great tidal pool; Daymer Bay on the other side of the estuary is often calm and good for swimming.

The walk starts near Oldtown Cove just next to the Camel Trail, an 18-mile cycle path between Padstow and Wenfordbridge. It's one of Cornwall's tourism success stories, with around half a million users a year. Just take care not to get mown down as you emerge onto the trail, as it really is a cyclists' superhighway!

It's best to start this walk around two hours before high tide. That way you will see the creek at its best, and the swim spots on the estuary will be full of water. Saying that, the wonderful thing about the tidal environment on this walk is that it is always in flux, and it is beautiful at all states of the tide.

The Camel Trail follows the route of an old railway line, so is flat and easy to walk. The track was originally laid in the 1890s, and visitors would have arrived from London by steam train from Waterloo. There is a wonderful description of this historic train service in *Atlantic Coast Express: From the Footplate* by Stephen Austin. When the train left Wadebridge, the scene would change: "Grey river mud gives way to golden sea sand, seen to best advantage at this time of day with autumn sunlight painting up the fields and farmhouses on the far bank. The fireman checks his fire… A man painting a boat in Oldtown Cove turns and waves as the train passes on the causeway behind him. Speed is reduced to 15mph for Little Petherick Creek Bridge, which consists of three 150ft trusses set on a curve… we coast into Padstow Station."

Now of course, the trains are long gone, tourists arrive by car, and the old line is home to cyclists and walkers. The first swim spot is in Oldtown Cove ❷, a delightful little beach with spectacular views

up the estuary to Bodmin Moor in the distance. It is lovely and sheltered, and there are usually boats moored there. Being two miles from Padstow, it is quiet, as most people pass by and don't realise it's there. It's a great place for your first dip, and you can have fun swimming to the boats and around the buoys.

The walk heads down the river along the Camel Trail to the Little Petherick Creek Bridge ❸, an impressive construction of iron girders which, by all accounts, was a real challenge for the engineers back in Victorian times. The iron for the construction arrived by train at Wadebridge and was then transported down the estuary on barges. Temporary staging was erected over the creek, and of course they had to work around the tides. The line between Wadebridge and Padstow was eventually opened in 1899, and trains ran until 1967, when the infamous Dr Beeching closed it.

Immediately after the bridge, you can drop down a small path on the left to a beach on the banks of the creek. This makes a spectacular swim spot with the dramatic setting of the bridge behind you. Take care if the tide is going out, as the water funnels under the bridge, and the outward current can be quite fast.

From the bridge, the walk continues along the trail until you reach a pond on your left. To the right here is Dennis Cove ❹, another swim spot in the beautiful waters of the Camel. After this, you head inland, and start to follow the Saints Way. This is a walking trail from Padstow on the north coast to Fowey on the south, which follows the probable route of early Christians making their way from Ireland and Wales to pilgrimage sites on the European mainland. It was created after local walkers found some forgotten granite stiles in

1984, and takes in several lovely old churches and Celtic crosses, as well as varied landscapes.

The route takes you to the summit of Dennis Hill, where the imposing Dennis Hill Obelisk  6 commands views in every direction. Known locally simply as 'the Monument' it was erected in 1889 to commemorate Queen Victoria's Golden Jubilee in 1887. From here you drop down with wonderful views to Little Petherick Creek below, stretching and narrowing as it extends inland.

You pass through the charming village of Little Petherick 10, which has a church dedicated to St Petroc, a Welsh prince who went to Ireland to become a monk. From Ireland he sailed to Cornwall, where he founded a monastery in Padstow (once St Petroc's Stowe). He then went on pilgrimage to Rome and Jerusalem, before returning 30 years later to Cornwall with his pet wolf. It is said that he wanted a more solitary, contemplative life and that the beautiful church is built on the site of his cell. It was described by Nikolaus Pevsner as "one of the architectural highlights of Cornwall". If you have the chance, go inside to appreciate the interior, which is not actually that old; the beautifully decorated rood screen and loft across the aisle were created between 1908 and 1947 by Gothic Revival architect Sir John Ninian Cooper.

The walk then crosses the creek and takes you back along the opposite bank, which is home to many interesting wading birds including herons, egrets and, most especially, curlews. The curlew is Britain's largest wading bird, with a distinctive long, curved beak, and is sadly in decline. Its call is haunting, a watery, wavery sound. Composer and ornithologist Peter Cowdrey describes it as having "a particular emotional appeal, evoking melancholy and ecstasy at the same time". If you are lucky you will both hear and see these magical birds.

Alongside the creek you will see a sign for Sea Mill (Sea Mills on the OS map). Built in the creek in the 17th century, the mill used the tidal waters to grind corn. It stopped operations in 1899, because the construction of the railway bridge across the end of the creek disrupted the tidal flow. There are no obvious mill remains, but as you get nearer to the sea you will see a house on the right 12. This is one of the old buildings that served the mill; opposite it is a large tidal enclosure where the mill was located.

You walk through a hamlet and descend back to the Camel Trail, with expansive views ahead of the estuary as it spreads out to the distant sea. Turn back along the trail inland, and maybe stop for a final dip in Oldtown Cove before arriving back at the car park.

DIRECTIONS

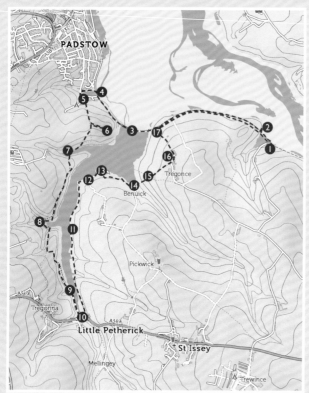

right-hand side of the pond. Follow it to where it reaches a track. Turn left at the track and follow it to reach a wooden gate with the Saints Way sign.
0.2 miles

⑤ Turn left onto the track between the driveway and the wooden gate, and follow the track as it bears around to the right, into a large field, and up the hill. Follow the Saints Way waymarkers to a stile at the top of the rise. Cross the stile and go through the metal gate to your left which leads to the obelisk.
0.3 miles

⑥ After a look round the obelisk to admire the views, return to the stile; turn left to follow the hedge downhill towards the creek into a large field. Bear right across the field to the hedge at the bottom, where there is a Saints Way sign leading you down into the woods.
0.3 miles

⑦ You reach a footbridge; cross it and follow the path uphill. Walk along the right-hand side of the field with the creek on your left. Turn right at the end and go through three fields and stiles, following the yellow arrow and the black cross Saints Way signs. You eventually descend to the creek edge from the corner of the last field.
0.6 miles

① From the car park, climb up the steps to the Camel Trail and turn left. Walk for a short distance, over the bridge, and you will see the first beach to your right. Look for a hole in the hedge to the right to descend.
0.2 miles

② After a dip in Oldtown Cove, rejoin the Camel Trail and continue in the direction of Padstow. You come to the distinctive metal Petherick Creek bridge; cross it and look for a

path left down to the shore of the creek for a swim.
0.9 miles

③ Return to the Camel Trail and keep going towards Padstow. You cross a small bridge with a pond on the left.
0.4 miles

④ Maybe pausing for a dip here at Dennis Cove on the right, just after passing the pond, take the small path off to the left that descends and skirts around the

⑧ Cross a boardwalk, and then follow the path uphill and to the right, still guided by the yellow

52

Saints Way signs, along a field edge. You reach a gate, turn left before it and walk along the right-hand edge of the field by the herringbone stone wall. Continue to follow the wall as it turns right, and then descend into the wood.
0.5 miles

9 You pass a wooden jetty on the left and grass with a sign saying 'Private property'. Carry straight on through the houses, past Upper Deck and The Anchorage on your left. You arrive at the centre of the village, meeting the main road.
0.2 miles

10 After a look around St Petroc church on your right, cross the bridge on the main road. Just after the bridge take the public footpath on the left that goes back along the other side of the creek. You cross a footbridge, then go through a field.
0.5 miles

11 You arrive at a stile signed 'Public Footpath Sea Mill': cross here to continue alongside the creek (if it is very muddy the path continues inland).
0.5 miles

12 You see a grey house on your right. Walk up to it and bear left, walking past the 'No Parking Turning Point' sign on the left. You reach a concrete public footpath sign on left, turn right here where it says 'Public Footpath'. The path moves away from the creek.
0.2 miles

13 Cross a stile and head right diagonally uphill across the field to the gap in the hedge at the top left hand corner of the field. In the next field, walk along the left hand border of the field. You reach a conifer hedge and at the end of this on the left is a stile; cross this and go down steps. Turn right through a gate.
0.2 miles

14 Turn left into the lane and head down the hill, passing a house called The Fort on the right, to reach the creek. Turn right here, cross a wooden footbridge and follow the footpath straight ahead through the field – when we did this it was full of maize which was higher than us.
0.1 miles

15 You reach a lane, which you cross over, and then cross the stile opposite. Go through another two fields, heading towards the hamlet.
0.2 miles

16 In the hamlet turn left down the lane, past Tregonce Farmhouse on the right and Swallow Barn on the left. Go past a sign saying 'Permissive path only' and follow the track downhill to the Camel Trail.
0.3 miles

17 On reaching the Camel Trail, turn right to make your way back to the car park.
1 mile

Walk 6

TRESCORE ISLANDS CIRCULAR

This wonderful walk along the wild and rugged north Cornish cliffs takes in a blue channel, islands and epic views down the coast. The swimming is best around high water, although still possible at lower tides.

INFORMATION

DISTANCE: 3.5 miles
TIME: Allow 3–4 hours
MAP: OS Explorer 106 Newquay and Padstow
START POINT: Car park in Porthcothan (SW 859 719, PL28 8LW).
END POINT: Car park in Porthcothan
PUBLIC TRANSPORT: A5 bus between Padstow and Newquay.
SWIMMING: Porthcothan Bay (SW 855 721), channel at Trescore Islands (SW 848 719) and Porth Mear Cove (SW 849 715).
PLACES OF INTEREST: Trescore Islands, Bronze Age cemetery at Park Head.
REFRESHMENTS: Porthcothan Bay Stores has tables outside where you can sit and eat a well-earned pasty (01841 520950, PL28 8LW). There's a tea room at Berryfields Holiday Park in the village, which has a good reputation for cream teas (01841 520178, PL28 8PW).
EASIER ACCESS: Unfortunately, the only access to Trescore Islands is by walking the coast path, although if you park at Atlantic View campsite it is a shorter, more level walk. There is swimming at Porthcothan right next to the car park – but go at high tide to avoid a long walk to the water!
NEARBY SWIM SPOTS: Treyarnon Bay has a beautiful tidal pool in the rocks, which is well worth a visit. It also has a spectacular cavern with an enormous pool inside, which can be visited at low tide by swimming or wading through the channel between the beach and Trethias Island – only advisable on a day when the sea is calm. Mawgan Porth has a spectacular sandy beach at low tide and is a fantastic place to play in the waves.

W ho can resist the lure of an island? Well on this adventure we have a little archipelago, and an idyllic swimming spot between the islands and the shore. It makes a magical yet safe swim safari, but it is important to point out that you need a very calm day with no wind if you want to swim out around the islands.

The walk starts in the small seaside village of Porthcothan ❶, the most southerly of the 'Seven Bays in Seven Days' that some tourism supremo dreamed up as a marketing slogan a while back. The seven bays referred to are along the coast south-west of Padstow: Trevone, Harlyn, Mother Ivey's, Booby's, Constantine, Treyarnon and finally Porthcothan. Each is beautiful, with its own special qualities, and worthy of a visit.

Porthcothan has a U-shaped beach that fills up at high tide and completely empties at low, leaving lots of little pools and caves to explore. You walk on the coast path past the main beach, and then pass a small cove that makes a lovely swim stop. It has the curious anchor-shaped remains of a rock islet called Jan Leverton's Island. The island had an arch and a 'window' until 2014, when a huge storm took a massive lump out of it. It's still fun to swim around when the tide is right. Talking of the tide, this walk, in terms of swim opportunities, is best done on a day with little wind, and around high water, as we shall see later. That said, the beach and the shoreline just south of it are fascinating to discover at low water, with rockpools, inlets and caves to explore.

Porthcothan has had a few famous literary residents in its time. D.H. Lawrence came here in 1916, just after his novel *The*

Rainbow had been published (and almost immediately banned). He stayed at Porthcothan House, a big property set back from the beach, which you can still rent out for holidays. He borrowed it from fellow writer J.D. Beresford, author of early science fiction and horror novels.

Lawrence described Porthcothan as "a cove of the sea where the waves are always coming in past jutty black rocks. It is a cove like Tristan sailed into from Lyonesse – just the same. It belongs to 2000 years back". Lawrence was referring here to the Arthurian legend of Tristan and Iseult, in which Lyonesse is a mythical country off Cornwall. He had probably read Swinburne's epic poem *Tristram of Lyonesse*, published in 1882.

In more recent times the village was home to the playwright and fisherman Nick Darke. He lived in a house by the beach with his wife Jane and two boys and very sadly died young, at the age of just 56. He was born and bred in Cornwall and many of his plays reflect that, exploring issues affecting Cornish people including tourism, mining and fishing. He and Jane, a film-maker, were fanatical beachcombers – an activity which is known in Cornwall as wrecking. As Jane (who still lives there) explains on her website, "A wreck breaks up, washes ashore, becomes wreckage. To take this is therefore 'wrecking'."

They loved to head out at the right state of the tide, finding flotsam and jetsam from all over the world, including tags from fellow lobster fishermen, whom Nick then contacted and made friends with. They made a fascinating film together about this called *The Wrecking Season*, and after Nick died, Jane made a film about his last months, called *The Art of Catching Lobsters*. Both films take you into their rugged world on the edge of the Atlantic and are worth searching out online.

Jane, who used to be a beach warden, is a passionate environmentalist, and is concerned about the impact of tourism on wildlife. Over many years she has observed the behaviour of visitors to Cornwall, and how they have not always respected the place. She is worried about what she describes as the tourist invasion, which she believes is causing the "wildlife and the wild places to be diminished, very fast". And it is true that we, as tourists, have a responsibility to the places we visit. We should not do anything harmful, and should take away nothing but photos and memories. We share our thoughts on this in the introduction to this book.

The walk takes you along the southern side of the beach and out onto the headland, where you pass a large blowhole. There are many on this part of the coast, as the sea constantly grinds away at the cracks in the caves. As you walk past the blowhole you will see Trescore Islands ❸ on the right, with a beautiful sheltered channel, Trescore Pool, between them and the shore. A stunning place to swim at high water, it dries out at low tide, leaving a sandy pool to wallow about in. It is home to a dazzling seaweed garden, and if you take a snorkel you will be rewarded with a kaleidoscope of colours, as well as numerous shoals of fish.

Jane Darke, in her book *Held by the Sea*, describes it as follows: "There's never a day when the islands are the same… there is life here, in abundance. The tiniest diatoms suspended in an April algal bloom. The fossilized corals embedded in the slate. The seaweeds with soft dark green fingers, red, translucent, palm-like fronds, bright green frills and weeds that are turquoise, green and pink all at the same time. The living shells, yellow flat winkles, pink cowries and netted dog whelks waving their

57

sea fan, its beautiful branches sticking out among the rest of the debris.

After this you climb up to Park Head ❺, from where there are grand views up and down the coastline. As you walk you will notice various mounds (marked as tumuli on the OS map). These are the remains of a Bronze Age cemetery. People were buried, in either single or multiple graves, in what are known as 'bowl barrows'. These are the mounds you can see, and they are listed by Historic England as a scheduled monument because of their national importance.

As you come off Park Head you will see Bedruthan Steps ❻ spread out before you, a line of impressive sea stacks that legend has it were used by the giant Bedruthan as stepping stones at high tide. However, the National Trust, which owns this part of the coastline, says this legend was probably invented by the Victorians, about the same time as the area started being visited by tourists. They would arrive at Newquay, and the cliffs above Bedruthan were perfect for them to visit by carriage. Apparently, the local farmer cashed in by offering stalls for the horses for a small sum.

In theory, you can visit the beach at Bedruthan by extending the walk slightly down the coast to the staircase down to the beach, but at the time of writing it is closed because of a rock fall, with no plans to reopen any time soon. Check on the National Trust website for the latest information.

The walk then takes you inland via fields and past attractive stone cottages. After this, you can either take a fully circular route back via the roads, or else do a loop back to the coast. The latter is probably advisable in the summer when the roads are busier, and also has the advantage of taking you past Trescore Islands again, where you can see them at a different state of the tide.

trunks… the shoals of tiny bass and grey mullet. The pipefish, a slender whip."

To get down to the water, walk along the coast path with the islands on your right until you are opposite their southern end. At this point you can walk down over the rocks. Someone (probably a fisherman) has even put down a bit of concrete to ease your way. Get into the water off the rocks, and enjoy the sensation of swimming in another world. If it's calm enough, you can swim around the islands, or simply enjoy exploring in and around the inlets.

The next part of the walk takes you down to Porth Mear ❹, a rocky beach which is mostly reef and has rockpools bristling with fish and other animals. Look out for clingfish, blennies and even sea slugs. Lots of stuff gets washed up here, and it's the only place we've ever found a

DIRECTIONS

1 Turn right out of the car park, then right onto the coast road and immediately left by the red phone box to follow the coast path up and to the left side of the beach.
0.1 miles

2 Follow the coast path with Porthcothan Beach on your right. Keep following the path around the headland at the end, passing a path down to the cove and potential swim spot and then taking care around a blowhole on your right. You will see Trescore Islands on your right. Keep walking parallel to the islands until the southerly end of the islands, then stop and make your way down the rocks to get to the water.
0.6 miles

3 After a swim in the channel between the shore and the Trescore Islands, return to the coast path and continue along to Porth Mear.
0.3 miles

4 After taking a swim or exploring the rockpools of the cove, continue south along the coast path to Park Head.
0.6 miles

5 From Park Head, walk alongside a stone herringbone wall on your left. At the end of the wall is a kissing gate with a wooden car park sign. There is also a sign for Mawgan Porth, pointing past the coves to the south.
0.4 miles

6 After admiring the view over Bedruthan Steps, turn left through the kissing gate, walk through three fields, and you will see some stone cottages ahead and a gate on the right with a wooden car park sign.
0.2 miles

7 Go through the gate and walk along the path. You arrive at a lane with a car park ahead (point **8**) on the opposite side. Here you have two options: first, a fully circular walk that includes some walking on roads, and second one that loops back to the coast path and avoids the roads.
0.1 miles

CIRCULAR OPTION

8 Turn right and walk along the lane with the car park on your left, to the road. At the road, turn left.
0.1 miles

9 Follow the road for Porthcothan all the way back to the start, keeping left past the brown Old MacDonald's Farm around the bend.
1.1 miles

OFF-ROAD OPTION

8 Turn left down the lane. Where it bends left by the house, head right through the five-bar gate, which has a National Trust sign saying 'Footpath to Porth Meor Beach and Park Head'. Follow the path to the left and down to Porth Meor Beach and then retrace the start of the walk to Porthcothan. The OS map shows a footpath leading from the house back towards Porthcothan instead, but this is no longer accessible – as we found!
1.6 miles

Walk 7

HOLYWELL BAY AND ST CUTHBERT'S WELL CIRCULAR

A magnificent walk taking in dunes and cliffs, wide sands and a narrow cove, a famously pink pub and a multi-coloured, mystical Cornish cave.

INFORMATION

DISTANCE: 5.5 miles
TIME: 5 hours
MAP: OS Explorer 104 Redruth and St Agnes
START POINT: National Trust car park in Holywell (SW 767 587, TR8 5DD).
END POINT: National Trust car park in Holywell.
PUBLIC TRANSPORT: Bus routes 85 and 87 between Newquay and Truro call at Holywell.
SWIMMING: Porth Joke (SW 771 605), Vugga Cove below the Bowgie Inn (SW 776 608).
PLACES OF INTEREST: St Cuthbert's Well, West Pentire poppy fields in May and June.
REFRESHMENTS: The Bowgie Inn has a great position on top of the cliffs at Crantock and is conveniently placed along the walk (01637 830363, TR8 5SE). The Treguth Inn in Holywell Bay is a dog-friendly, traditional thatched hostelry serving good value pub grub (01637 830248, TR8 5PP).
EASIER ACCESS: Holywell Bay is a 5-minute flat walk from the start point; you could park at the Bowgie Inn (point 10) and walk down a gentle hill to the cove below (make sure it's high tide, as it's not so swimmable at low).
NEARBY SWIM SPOTS: Surfing at Fistral Bay in Newquay; swimming and cave exploring at Trevaunance Cove, St Agnes.

*H*olywell Bay **2**, with its acres of golden sands and distinctive twin islands offshore, is well known, not least because it featured heavily in the latest series of *Poldark*. Countless trysts, fights and gatherings were staged here, which isn't surprising given the dramatic beauty of the beach. You'll need to do this walk at low tide if you want to see the extraordinary St Cuthbert's Well, which you really shouldn't miss.

The village of Holywell is pretty forgettable, with quite a lot of new houses being built, but you soon leave it behind as you cross the stream and head onto the beach, which is huge. At low water there can be strong currents, so don't swim here, but wait until you get to the next bay.

The beach gets its name from St Cuthbert's Well **3**, a holy well in a cave on the northern side of the beach. It's a natural feature, but once you see it you will realise why it's been ascribed supernatural powers, as it really looks very different from most other caves in Cornwall.

To find it, once you're on the main beach, with the sea in front of you, head right, towards the cliffs at the north of the beach. The slanted opening to the cave is near the low-water mark and has a large wooden post in it on the right, no doubt washed up some time ago and wedged there ever since. If you can't find it, ask someone, but there are often people gathered around the entrance.

To see the holy well, you have to climb up a little set of ancient steps to the left of the cave opening, where you will come upon a cascade of naturally occurring ledges, each with a little pool of water, like a series of baptismal fonts. There is a natural spring inside the cave and water trickles down through the pools. There is a fresh yet salty smell, probably from the minerals in the rock.

The colours are breathtaking, a range of reds, pinks, greys and browns, and the whole thing is like some fantasy grotto.

In 1894, siblings Mabel and Lillian Quiller-Couch published a book called *Ancient and Holy Wells of Cornwall*, describing how they went on a 'sacred pilgrimage' of all the sites. This is what they had to say about St Cuthbert's Well: "This well has Nature for its architect, no mark of man's hand being seen in its construction; a pink enamelled basin, filled by drippings from the stalactitic roof, forms a picture of which it is difficult to describe the loveliness. What wonder then, that the simple folk around should endow it with mystic virtues?"

The cave is said to be named after St Cuthbert of Lindisfarne. According to legend, his relics were being transported from the North East to Ireland to escape the warring Vikings, when the party got blown off course. They somehow temporarily ended up in the cave, where they touched it with the saint's spiritual powers. For centuries people have gone to the cave to take its holy waters, hoping to be healed of all manner of ailments.

After visiting the cave, you head up a steep sandy path through the dunes ❹ and onto the cliffs known as the Kelseys. At the front of Kelsey Head you can see the remains of an Iron Age fort, with a bank and ditch ❺. It is listed as a scheduled monument by Historic England, which describes it as a 'cliff castle', and notes there are only about 60 such castles in the country, 40 of which are in Cornwall. It was probably constructed around the time of Christ, and would have been occupied by someone of high status who wanted to be in a strong defensive position.

Just off the headland is a little island called The Chick, where you can often see seals. You then head down the cliffs to see Porth Joke ❻ coming

up on your left. Also known locally as Polly Joke, this is a wonderful U-shaped beach with lots of caves. There are many stories about how it got its local name, but most seem to favour the theory that it comes from the Cornish name Pol Lejouack, meaning Jackdaw Pool (or water generally).

It's never that crowded, as it doesn't have a car park, and it is a stunning swim spot. There are usually big rollers which are fun to jump in, and it's also a good place for body surfing. Around two hours after low tide a rather lovely pool forms in a channel between the rocks at the northern end of the beach. It's an oasis of calm after the waves.

After swimming, and no doubt snacking, it's time to head up the beach and continue north along the coast path through West Pentire ❼. In May and June people come from all around to see a magnificent display of poppies and corn marigolds here; a striking combination of red and yellow flowers in great profusion. The land is managed by the National Trust, which also sows some of the land with barley, to benefit birds such as the corn bunting and mammals such as the brown hare.

The walk takes you around the headland towards the lovely beach of Crantock. Just before heading up to the Bowgie Inn there is a small inlet off to the left ❽. With lots of rocky platforms and ledges, this is a fun place to swim at high tide, or just to sit a while on the rocks and enjoy the views.

The pink-painted Bowgie Inn ❾ is a bit of an institution locally. Owned by the same family for the last 45 years, it has an enviable position on the cliffs, and its car park often plays host to classic vehicle gatherings. This does make it rather popular, not to say heaving, in summer months.

At this point on the walk we turn inland. Before the walk leaves the village, you will notice a small shed on the right, with a sign bearing the legend 'John Sleep Gramophones' ❿. John is a former chemistry teacher who started repairing wind-up gramophones and phonographs 25 years ago because he wanted something to do when he retired. His shed is packed to the gunnels with wonderful gramophone players, many with enormous trumpets. The walls are lined with old 78 records, which he also sells. He is one of the few enthusiasts who still work on these old machines, and people send them to him from all over the world. He is a delightful chap and will be very happy to show you his incredible workshop and have a chat.

The walk heads down a lane and then across the fields and back to Holywell Bay. If you started the walk at low tide, so as to see St Cuthbert's Well, the tide will now be well on its way in and so there's the chance for another well-earned swim!

DIRECTIONS

❶ From the car park, cross the road and take the footpath leading right, following the sign for the beach and coast path. Pass to the left of St Piran's Inn and then bear right across the grassy/sandy area towards the dunes.
0.2 miles

❷ Cross the footbridge and turn left, walking around the dunes on your right to the beach. Once on the open sands, head towards the right-hand side, to find St Cuthbert's Well near the low-tide line.
0.7 miles

❸ From St Cuthbert's Well, head back along the beach with the cliffs on your left.
0.2 miles

❹ Where the cliffs end and the dunes begin, turn left up a steep sandy path to the top, where you'll find a wooden kissing gate to the left and 'The Kelseys' National Trust sign. Go through the gate and follow the path around to the headland.
0.8 miles

❺ After exploring the Iron Age embankment at Kelsey Head or checking for seals on The Chick, follow the coast path with the beach on your left down to the sand (you could also descend over rocks about halfway between the headland and the top of the bay).
0.6 miles

❻ Porth Joke beach is a perfect spot for a swim. Then from the top of the beach, with the sea behind you, turn left and follow the path. Almost immediately, it splits: go left each time, and follow the path around the headland.
0.6 miles

7 As you round West Pentire headland you will see Crantock beach ahead and to your left. Keep following the path as it descends. You can turn left off the path before you ascend to the Bowgie Inn, to find a cute little inlet which is good for swimming at high tide.
0.2 miles

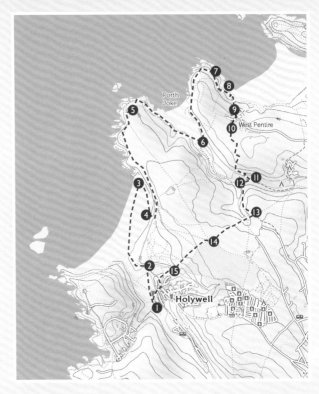

8 From the inlet, continue on the coast path then turn up the tarmac path, following signs for the Bowgie Inn and a sign that says 'Conservation Area'. Follow the path uphill past granite pillars and a car park to the left to the Inn.
0.1 miles

9 From the Bowgie Inn, turn right out of the main (village) entrance, and right again signed to the car park. Turn left where the road bends right, following a blue P sign and a green public footpath sign.
0.1 miles

10 Pass the gramophone workshop on your right and the car park on the left and follow the track. At the first bend left keep following the track as it zig-zags on and then diverts right onto a path over a footbridge at the end, just before buildings ahead.
0.5 miles

11 You reach a kissing gate. Go through and turn right. Follow the track to just before the car park.
0.1 miles

12 Take the track on the left-hand side before the car park. Walk until the path forks, keep left and follow the path as it bends left.
0.1 miles

13 You reach a T-junction with a sign post. Turn right for Holywell, the path then forks and you take the right fork.
0.3 miles

14 You reach a five-bar gate on the right. Go through it and turn immediately left, following the path along the wall and fence on your left, with the dunes ahead. You reach a kissing gate, go through it following the sign for Holywell, and continue down the path with the golf course on your left.
0.5 miles

15 Cross a stream by a gate that says 'Private' and just after, scramble left up the sandy path. Turn left at the top by a big modern house and follow the path inland between the houses. When you get to the main road, turn right and follow the road down to the car park.
0.1 miles

Walk 8

ST AGNES AND
CHAPEL PORTH CIRCULAR

A cativating walk through Cornwall's mining history along cliff tops and around coves, as well as up to the summit of St Agnes Beacon, one of the highest spots on the north Cornish coast.

INFORMATION

DISTANCE: 8.5 miles
TIME: All day
MAP: OS Explorer 104 Redruth and St Agnes
START POINT: Car park near Wheal Kitty (SW 726 512 nearest postcode: TR5 0RJ).
END POINT: Car park near Wheal Kitty.
PUBLIC TRANSPORT: Bus routes 87 and 224 from Truro and Newquay and 315 from Redruth serve St Agnes.
SWIMMING: Trevellas Porth (SW 725 519), Trevaunance Cove (SW 722 516) and Chapel Porth (SW 696 496).
PLACES OF INTEREST: St Agnes Beacon, Wheal Coates Mine, Blue Hills Tin Mine.
REFRESHMENTS: The Driftwood Spars pub in Trevaunance Cove is an award-winning pub with its own brewery (01872 552591, TR5 0RT). The Chapel Porth Beach Café is a great little place with lovely staff, and its 'iced hedgehogs' ice creams are well worth a try (01872 552487, TR5 0NS).
EASIER ACCESS: Trevaunance Cove and Chapel Porth both have car parks in front of them; Trevaunance is an easy walk down the slipway, while getting to the beach at Chapel Porth from the car park involves a very short walk over sometimes rough ground.
NEARBY SWIM SPOTS: The tidal pool at Porthtowan (right-hand side of the beach) is a bit of a legendary spot for wild swimmers, though it does involve a tricky climb down the rocks. Perranporth also has a tidal pool, as well as being a great surf beach.

The walk is best started a couple of hours before low tide, and starts high on the cliffs above Trevaunance and Trevellas Coves. The area around St Agnes has a really rich mining history, and you can see its legacy across the parish in the form of chimneys and other buildings. The abandoned engine houses on the cliffs now evoke an atmosphere of rugged romance, but for those who worked in them during the tin industry's heyday in St Agnes, between the 1830s and 1870s, they were often miserable places.

The walk takes you down a lane to the pretty valley of Trevellas Combe, which leads to the first beach on the walk. On the right you will see the Blue Hills Tin Mine ❷, the only place producing tin in this country today. It is open to visitors and you can do a self-guided tour and find out more about the process.

You walk along the valley to arrive at Trevellas Porth ❸, a beautifully wild beach with an enormous reef. Completely exposed at low tide, this is full of fascinating rockpools and, even more excitingly for the swimmer, some entrancing larger, swimmable pools and gullies. To find them, you need to be at the beach around low tide. You cross the reef (it is a good idea to wear wetsuit shoes) and head to the right-hand side. A large lagoon opens up, and a deep channel which leads to further calm pools overlooked by two dramatic rock stacks. These pools make for a magical swim, as the water is often an intense azure colour, while the more adventurous can indulge in a bit of jumping and diving – after checking the depth, of course. This beach is also a great snorkelling spot.

From Trevellas Porth, it's a steep climb up to the clifftop, where you may notice a plaque to the Motor Cycling Club. Once a year,

on Easter Saturday, the cliffside is full of motor-bikes scrambling along the rough track as part of the Lands' End Trial, which has been going for over a hundred years and is described as an 'auto-motive eccentricity'. So maybe avoid the Easter weekend unless you're a motorbike fan!

The walk leads down to Trevaunance Cove ❺, passing through Down Quay Gardens, a good place to stop for a rest and admire the view. The beach is popular with surfers, and on the right you will see the reef that links up to Trevellas Cove. On the left-hand side of the beach you may notice many square, geometric rocks scattered about. These are what is left of a stone jetty, and if you look carefully along the cliffs on the left-hand side you will see the remains of buildings.

There used to be a whole harbour here, built along the cliffs. In fact, five harbours have been constructed here since the 17th century, all of which were washed away in storms, the latest in 1920. They served both the fishing and the mining industries, and some interesting, though rather faded, display boards show fascinating old black and white pictures of the harbour at work. Wooden gantries were erected at the top of the cliffs, which would connect down to the harbour and ships below to transport cargo from the ships to the shore.

After visiting the beach, and perhaps having a play in the surf, you head uphill and past a rather unusual collection of cedar-clad houses, which bring to mind the work of the American architect Frank Lloyd-Wright. They were constructed around 2014 and are cleverly built into the hillside, without overlooking each other. With huge glass windows, they certainly look like luxury homes.

You ascend past the houses and emerge onto lanes with beautiful views back down to Trevau-nance Cove and Trevellas Porth. You start to head inland and the environment gradually changes as you continue up towards St Agnes Beacon ⓬. This famous trig point is in the middle of a wonderful area of moorland, covered with gorse and heather, which is a riot of yellow and purple in high summer. At 189 metres, it commands the most incredible panoramic views, including 30 miles out to sea on a clear day.

A circular metal toposcope plaque inserted into the top of the stone monument lists all that you can see, including Nancekuke Airfield (the big white balloon), Carn Brea, St Ives Head and Gull Rock at Portreath. It also contains some interesting infor-mation, including the legend of the child-eating giant Bolster, who was said to be able to stand with one foot on St Agnes Beacon and the other on Carn Brea, about six miles away. The plaque also explains how his unfortunate wife was made to clear all the fields of stones and carry them up to the top of the hill in her apron, until St Agnes tricked the giant to his death.

This legend is re-enacted every year, on the first May bank holiday weekend, in a colourful ceremony called the Bolster Pageant. The night before, there is a torchlight procession from the village to the Beacon where a bonfire is lit, and clay houses are set on fire. Then at noon the following day people gather in the village with enormous puppets, including an 8.5-metre effigy of the giant himself, and process to the sound of beating drums along the cliffs to Chapel Porth beach. It's a great spectacle.

Chapel Porth ⓰ is in fact the next stop on the walk, a beautiful spot offering many intriguing caves with beautiful red and pink rocky interiors. The beach is best explored at low tide, but keep an eye on the time because the incoming tide really races in. From the beach you will see the iconic Wheal Coates tin mine ⓱ on the cliffs above. As the National Trust, which manages the area, puts it: "The image of the Towanroath Shaft engine house, famous on postcards, calendars and on the telly, represents for many the serene beauty of the north Cornish coast. In reality this industrial landscape holds a harsh and austere history."

The mine opened in 1802 and was worked until 1889. Its operations extended out under the sea bed, and the engine house you see on the cliffs was used to pump water out of the deeper levels of the mine. The conditions for the miners were very tough; they worked deep underground in cramped and stifling conditions, and many were killed or injured by explosions, rock falls, and becoming entangled in machinery. Gazing up at the engine house from the sands below, the mine ruin feels like a gravestone or memorial.

As you leave the beach, make sure you visit the café, which is a bit of an institution. It's been run by the same family for 35 years, and their unique speci-

ality is iced hedgehogs. This is a cone full of vanilla ice cream, topped with clotted cream and then rolled in honey-roasted hazelnuts. It was invented by the owner one day, when he was making brittle and overdid the nuts, and is a truly indulgent treat which provides much-needed energy for the hike back up the cliffs to the coast path.

Once up on the clifftops, you will soon come across the rest of Wheal Coates, which isn't visible from the beach below, and marvel at the extent of the site. The biggest building is the whim engine house and beside it is the ruin of the stamping engine, built earlier. The whim engine helped raise ore from Towanroath Shaft (which is further down the cliff) and also powered the crushing stamp. A little further on are the remains of the calciner building, where impurities such as arsenic were extracted from the ore. This mine would have been a hive of industry in its heyday, and it is said that the ghosts of miners who died here haunt the site, as well they might.

The walk continues around the windswept St Agnes Head ⓲ and below the lookout for the National Coastwatch Institution, where volunteer coastguards watch over the seas below to help keep seafarers safe. Look out for gannets and dolphins: these cliffs are a great place to watch them from. You'll notice a couple of islets to the north, which are called Bawden Rocks, or Cow and Calf, or Man and his Man. Here it seems the giant Bolster also had an influence, as legend has it he threw the rocks out to sea in a fit of pique. These small islands are home to nesting birds including guillemots, razorbills and puffins.

You descend back to Trevaunance Cove, where you can indulge in a well-earned stop in one of the many hostelries before the climb back up to the car park.

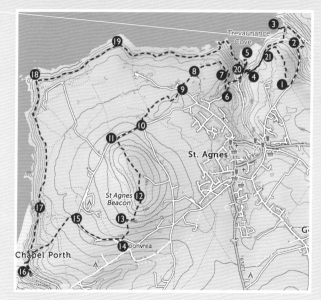

Polberro. Take this path, do not be put off by the 'Little Orchard Cottage private entrance' sign. The path continues uphill and there are great views down to the sea on the right. Pass Newman's Memorial Garden on your right.
0.2 miles

7 Just after the garden there is a T junction with a car park opposite. Turn right here and keep going up hill, following the track as it turns into a lane and bends to the left.
0.2 miles

8 You reach a chimney on your right. Go straight on here, ignoring the path to the right, and bear left by the green postbox.
0.2 miles

1 From the car park, with your back to the sea, turn left and walk along the lane downhill. There is a sharp hairpin bend to the right, and shortly after this a bridge.
0.4 miles

2 Just over the bridge, opposite the sign for Blue Hills Tin Mine, turn left onto the footpath signposted 'Perranporth 3 miles'. Follow the path to the sea.
0.2 miles

3 From Trevellas Porth beach, with your back to the sea, take the narrow footpath to the right just by the red lifebelt. It's a steep climb up to the top of the cliff. Once at the top, carry on with the sea on your right and then start to descend.
0.5 miles

4 Turn right at the green gate, down a zig-zag path which passes through Down Quay Gardens, with benches. The path comes out on a road by the public loos – turn right here and follow the slipway down to the beach.
0.2 miles

5 From Trevaunance Cove beach, walk back up the road past the loos on the left. Take the first road right, opposite the Driftwood Spars pub. Pass the Crib Shack and a red postbox on your right. Follow the road uphill, ignoring the footpath signposted to Chapel Porth, as it bends left and then right.
0.3 miles

6 You will see a public footpath on the right signposted to

9 You reach a T junction with the road with a sign saying 'Public Byway Polberro'. Cross the road and carry straight over onto a narrow path. Follow it, ignoring a track to the left, until you bend right and reach a junction of paths; turn left here. You reach a T-junction with a track; turn left following the red arrow on the wooden post. Follow this track as it bends right (ignoring right-hand turn for 'Cowling Cottage Private') and pass houses on your right including the Old Chapel.
0.4 miles

10 At a T-junction with Beacon Road, turn right. Walk along the road for a short distance and you will see a bench on the left.
0.2 miles

⓫ Immediately after the bench take the uphill path to the left leading onto the moorland. Keep straight on over a crossroads of paths and then bear right at the fork, just after the shaft on your right. You will now see the Beacon summit up ahead; continue to walk to it, ignoring other crossing paths.
0.4 miles

⓬ From St Agnes Beacon, continue south on the path, going downhill. The path bends right.
0.2 miles

⓭ Just after the path bends right, you take the second path to the left; you're essentially continuing straight downhill. (Do not go through the wooden gate into the field – if you get to the gate you have gone too far, turn back and take the first path right). After passing a mine shaft on your left, you reach a track where you turn right.
0.1 miles

⓮ You arrive at a road. Turn right here and follow the road.
0.4 miles

⓯ You arrive at a green National Trust sign saying Wheal Coates. Turn in here, walk through the car park to the pay machines at the end and follow the path, not to the mine (that's for later), but down to the car park at Chapel Porth beach.
0.6 miles

⓰ From Chapel Porth beach, head back up and take the coast

path bearing off to the left, heading back towards St Agnes.
0.5 miles

⓱ You reach Wheal Coates mine, a great place to explore. Then keep following the coast path as it hugs the cliffs with the sea on your left.
0.9 miles

⓲ You reach St Agnes Head. Keep following the coast path.
0.6 miles

⓳ You pass Newlands Head. Keep left, following the path close to the sea, ignoring any paths to the right. You descend towards Trevaunance Cove and follow the path as it bends right past some houses overlooking the cove, then past the telephone box and in front of the

houses, until it brings you out at the road down to the beach.
1.1 miles

⓴ Cross the road and, just to the right of the loos, rejoin the path you previously took, which takes you back up through the garden to the coast path. Turn left up the coast path, retracing your steps.
0.3 miles

㉑ Fork right by the 'Unfenced cliff ahead' sign, and then shortly after take the path to the right to skirt a small grey slag heap to the right, heading south. You reach a T-junction of tracks; turn left here and then shortly after take the grassy path to the right where you will see the engine house ahead. Follow this back to the car park.
0.4 miles

Walk 9

CARN MARTH QUARRIES CIRCULAR

A fascinating walk back through time, around a series of curiosities all related to the area's rich mining history. These include an open-air church, an amphitheatre and two refreshing quarry pools.

INFORMATION

DISTANCE: 3.5 miles
TIME: Allow 4 hours with swims and a picnic
MAP: OS Explorer 104 Redruth and St Agnes
START POINT: Entrance to Gwennap Pit (SW 717 417, TR16 5HH) where there is space for four cars.
END POINT: Entrance to Gwennap Pit.
PUBLIC TRANSPORT: Bus route 47 from Camborne and Truro stops in St Day (1 mile away), the nearest station is Redruth (2 miles away).
SWIMMING: Carn Marth Pool (SW 716 408), lower quarry (SW 723 409).
PLACES OF INTEREST: Gwennap Pit, Carn Marth open-air theatre, Figgy Dowdy's Well, Baronet's Engine House.
REFRESHMENTS: The Lanner Inn (01209 215611, TR16 6EH), The Coppice Inn (01209 315695, TR16 6JB) and Portreath Bakery (01209 314613, TR16 6HJ) are all in Lanner village. For something truly unique, Carn Brea Castle is now a restaurant serving Jordanian cuisine (01209 218358, TR16 6SL).
EASIER ACCESS: There are a few parking spaces by the open-air theatre, from where it is a short walk up a stony track to the main swim spot at Carn Marth (SW 715 406).
NEARBY SWIM SPOTS: There are lovely beaches at Portreath and Porthtowan, and it is worth checking out the tidal pool at Porthtowan.

The starting point for this walk is a truly remarkable feature called Gwennap Pit ❶, a conical amphitheatre first created when the surface collapsed into a mine hundreds of years ago. During the 18th and early 19th century, this parish was the richest copper mining district in Cornwall, and indeed it was even called the "richest square mile in the Old World".

John Wesley, the father of Methodism, took advantage of the natural acoustics and used the pit as a place to preach. He liked it so much, he returned 18 times between 1762 and 1789, drawing a crowd of 32,000 to one of his gatherings. When you think the population of Cornwall at the time was about 125,000 people, that's a really impressive number. He described the spot as "the most magnificent spectacle this side of heaven" and while that's quite a bold claim, it's definitely worth a look.

Following his death, the pit continued to be used for religious assemblies, and the 12 circular terraces were cut as seats by local miners between 1803 and 1806, in tribute to Wesley. Today it stands as a memorial to the Methodist movement across the country in the 18th century and remains a place of spiritual and historical significance. Services are held here throughout the summer months, and a large Methodist rally has taken place here every Whit Monday since 1807.

The pit can seat around 1,500 people in its rings and is also used for music and drama events, as well as weddings and even charity walks. Apparently if you walk around all 12 tiers from the top to the bottom and back again, you will have walked a mile, and children (but sadly not adults…) can receive a certificate if they complete it. In 2006 the pit became part of the Cornwall and West Devon Mining Landscape UNESCO World Heritage Site.

The walk follows bridleways and paths up onto Carn Marth ❹, a spectacular ancient hilltop blanketed in gorse, bracken, heath and wildflowers. It's a great place to see birds, including warblers, cuckoos, buzzards and peregrines. We also spotted swallows as we arrived at the first quarry for a swim. Carn Marth Pool (or the Cornish Granite and Freestone Quarry) once provided granite for a number of prominent buildings around Redruth. Stone from the various quarries in the area was also used for gravestones, monuments and the Redruth Viaduct.

It's a lovely spot, with banks dropping down to refreshing waters where islands are waiting to be conquered. A group of young boys were jumping into the water, encouraging us to join them, while fishermen set up camp on the opposite bank attempting to catch carp. Apparently, there are around 30 in the quarry, which were released in the waters some years back, including an elusive 30-pounder. In the summer when we visited, the water was warm and inviting, and only the promise of a second swim pulled us away.

Leaving the quarry it's worth pausing to take in the spectacular views. This is the highest point in the area, and on a clear day you can see for miles, including the Celtic Sea to the north and the English Channel to the south. If you have time, you can walk around to the trig point, from where you should be able to see Portreath on the north coast and across to Carn Brea, with a monument and castle, in the west. Basset Monument is a 27-metre granite obelisk that was built in 1836 in honour of Francis Basset, the head of an important mining family in the area.

Once you have taken in the views, the walk continues to another fascinating quarry, this one housing an open-air theatre ❺. Back in 1986, the Carn Marth Trust was set up in response to the threat of quarrying returning to the hill. They purchased the land and decided to convert the lower quarry into an open-air theatre. Since the very first production held here (*The Three Musketeers* by Cornwall Theatre Company), the quarry theatre has hosted concerts and annual productions by renowned Cornish theatre companies including Kneehigh and Miracle Theatre. Local stonemason Roger Eslick built the tiered seating, while the quarry now even has electricity on site. It's well worth looking out for a production here in the summer months – or why not stage your own spontaneous show while you are there?

Very close to the entrance to the quarry you might be able to find some steps leading down to an old well, known as either Figgy Dowdy's Well or Margery Daw's Well (after the nursery rhyme character). Young girls would bring their dolls here to be baptised in the water every Good Friday. There was even a local rhyme: 'Figgy Dowdy had a well/ On the top of Carn Marth Hill/ And she locked it up night and day/ Lest people carry the water away.' Margery/Figgy may have been a real person, whose job was to protect the well when it was the main water source for the nearby village. Figgy Dowdy is also the name of a pudding made with raisins, popular in the 18th century and often cooked on ships, as all of the ingredients have long life spans.

As you leave the quarry, you can see the chimney and ruins of Baronet's Engine House ❻, which was built on top of Pennance Mine (originally called Wheal Amelia). It was later renamed Pennance Consols to make it sound far

grander and attract money from naïve investors upcountry. Unfortunately for those financiers, the mine produced just 590 tons of copper between 1866 and 1872. This was considered such a small amount at the time that the locals referred to it as Wheal Bloody Nose, to make fun of the shareholders who saw little or no return. You can safely explore the historic engine house, with its impressively large chimney, which once powered the pumping engine.

It's now a five- to ten-minute walk to the next pool, which is easy to miss. Look out for a small track off to your left from the path you are following. Overgrown and smelling of honeysuckle, it suddenly reveals an unexpectedly enchanting quarry ❾. Sometimes known as the lower quarry, more poetically named Cathedral Quarry due to its high, sheer walls, it's a magical spot for a swim from the natural granite steps and platforms into the refreshing waters. Gorse and heather top the walls, and it feels like a place where something legendary should have happened. It is certainly a place people have been coming to for a long time: graffiti carved into a wall on the right of the quarry dates back to the 1930s.

The walk then returns back down to the village through more pleasant lanes and bridleways. You may want to visit Lanner, where there are a couple of pubs and a bakery selling great pasties. The quiet little village has an unexpected claim to fame, as experimental techno maverick Richard David James – better known as Aphex Twin – grew up here. He even produced a song called *Carn Marth*, and during the Cornish free party scene of the late 1980s, he put on raves in secret coves and in Gwennap Pit itself. With entrance donations taken in cannabis, we are fairly sure that John Wesley would not have approved.

DIRECTIONS

1 With Gwennap Pit behind you, turn right and walk along the road past Cathedral Farm on your right.
0.3 miles

2 Just after Trevethan Meadows on your left, turn right following the public bridleway sign. You reach a crossroads of paths, where you go straight on, as the bridleway turns into a path. You reach another crossroads, with a post with three blue arrows; again, go straight on.
0.4 miles

3 At another crossroads with a ruined building on the left, turn right and look out for the quarry pool on your left ahead.
0.2 miles

4 After your dip in Carn Marth Pool, take the rough path from the south-east side of the pool down to the main track. Turn right and walk along the track, which has whitish stones. The track bends around to the right and shortly after you will see a large metal gate off to the right. Turn through the gate to the quarry.
0.3 miles

5 Explore Carn Marth amphitheatre and Figgy Dowdy's Well before returning to the track. Keep going right along the track, you will soon have a fine view of an old engine house up ahead. The entrance to the site is on the right as you approach the building.
0.2 miles

6 After a look around Baronet's Engine House, come back out and face towards where you came from. Take the path right marked 'Mining Trail' with the orange sign, going to the right of Rockfield Farm, following the post with the red metal square on it. You reach a fork that has a wooden post with a blue arrow and an orange Mining Trail sign; go right here and pass Carn Marth House and Barn on your right.
0.6 miles

7 You reach a junction with a track and paths. This can be confusing. You need the stony path uphill, which is the middle one of three options to your left as you stand at the entrance to the

junction. After about 5 minutes' walk look for a small path through a thicket to the left. This takes you to the second swim.
0.3 miles

8 From the quarry pool retrace your steps to the footpath, turning left and carrying on walking. You reach a T-junction with a wooden post with blue arrows. Turn left here and go past a sign on the left saying 'No public right of way for vehicles'. Pass a cottage on your right.
0.3 miles

9 Take the path to right, where there is a wooden post with yellow arrows. You reach a crossroads that has a post with three blue arrows, on the path you originally took from Gwennap Pit. Turn right here and retrace your steps back to the start.
0.8 miles

Walk 10

PORTREATH AND
TEHIDY COUNTRY PARK CIRCULAR

A picturesque walk through Cornwall's mining history, taking you from windswept clifftops to magical woodland, with plenty of local legends and some unique swimming spots along the way.

INFORMATION

DISTANCE: 5.5 miles
TIME: 6 hours with stops
MAP: OS Explorer 104 Redruth and St Agnes
START POINT: Tehidy Country Park North Cliffs car park (SW 640 437, TR14 0TW).
END POINT: Tehidy Country Park North Cliffs car park.
PUBLIC TRANSPORT: Bus route 46 from Camborne serves Tehidy Country Park. Camborne station is a 45-minute walk.
SWIMMING: Portreath, including Lady Basset's Baths and Rocky Pool (SW 654 455), possibly at Basset's Cove if it is reopened (SW 638 442).
PLACES OF INTEREST: Lady Basset's Baths, Nancekuke Common, Minerals Tramway Heritage Project, Tehidy Country Park.
REFRESHMENTS: The Hub on the seafront in Portreath is great for coffee and cakes (01209 844666, TR16 4NN). The Portreath Arms on the Square is an ideal spot for a beer or even a spot of lunch (01209 842259, TR16 4LA). Finally, the Tehidy Country Park Café, in the park itself (01209 610094, TR14 0HA).
EASIER ACCESS: Park next to the beach at Portreath, with ramp access to the sands at the harbour end of the car park. Also Blue Badge parking.
NEARBY SWIM SPOTS: At Porthtowan scramble across the rocks to the right for a tidal pool that is filled up on each high tide. Perranporth has a tidal pool and a dramatic rock arch at the southern end of the beach.

This walk begins with a stroll from the car park down a road and onto a track that takes you to Basset's Cove. The Basset family name will crop up several times throughout today's adventure. They were some of the earliest Norman settlers in England, holding the land and manor at Tehidy from the 12th century, and they became extraordinarily wealthy in the 18th century by granting leases to exploit the tin and copper reserves under the land. They owned two of Cornwall's most profitable mines, Cooks Kitchen Mine in Pool and the nearby Dolcoath, which was dubbed 'The Queen of the Cornish Mines'. Basset's Cove ❷ was once used as a stone quarry, with horse-powered winding gear carrying the rocks up the cliff. It was also used to raise the wreckage of many of the ships that sank off this treacherous stretch of coast and, if rumours are to be believed, a great deal of illicit alcohol.

When we visited, the beach was closed due to cliff erosion. It can apparently be reached from Porthcadjack Cove and Mirrose Well Cove to the east, and at low water from Deadman's Cove and Greenbank Cove to the west. As you walk, you'll spot Samphire Island out at sea, where wild rock samphire was once harvested. The other rocks are unnamed on the OS map, but known as Carvannel Island and Asparagus Island; nesting seabirds make their seasonal homes on all. You'll also pass Porthcadjack Cove ❸, which people do access by scrambling down a steep scree slope, although there has been lots of rockfall here recently. Old ropes have been tied to the steepest parts to help you with the vertiginous descent and the breath-stealing climb back up.

Once you have followed the coast path down and up the steep valley, it bears inland through a field (away from its now-unsafe original route), before returning to the sheer edge of the cliffs. You are now above Ralph's Cupboard ❹, a curiously named and completely inaccessible collapsed sea cave. Some say the name comes from that of a smuggler who would hide his contraband behind its sheltering, door-like cliffs. Another legend says it was once the home of a giant known as the Wrath of Portreath, with the 'wrath' possibly corrupted to 'Ralph'. He was said to hurl rocks at passing boats, steal their cargo and eat their crew. Today the area is home to a colony of grey seals, with Ralph's Cupboard providing a safe haul-out for the marine mammals. The outcrop of rock dividing the Cupboard from the wider Western Cove is known as The Horse.

The path now leads out onto the headland from where you can see the golf-ball-shaped radar antenna of Remote Radar Head Portreath, on Nancekuke Common. Operated by the Royal Air Force, it provides long-range coverage of the south-western approach to the United Kingdom. As RAF Portreath it was a Fighter Command station during the Second World War, then during the 1950s it was used as a secret base for chemical weapons manufacture, producing the nerve agent sarin for laboratory test purposes. In 2000 it was reported that former employees of the base had died as a result of exposure to the nerve gas, while *The Independent* newspaper alleged that toxic materials had been dumped in nearby mineshafts. A large clean-up operation was mounted as a precautionary measure, but no toxic residues were discovered.

Below the giant golf ball, you should be able to spot a daymark on top of North Cliff, which is known locally as the Pepperpot. It was built

in 1846, when Portreath was Cornwall's most important port, shipping copper and coal in and out, and it served as both a navigational aid for ships and a coastguard lookout. You'll also see Gull Rock out at sea, and Portreath Pier with its iconic Monkey Hut (or House) on the end, which dates back to the 1900s. During storms, this was used as a shelter for harbour pilots, who would use flags or lanterns to guide ships safely in, or warn them away if conditions were too rough. The hut was washed away by Storm Hercules in January 2014, but it and other damaged parts of the harbour were rebuilt at a cost of £250,000.

If the tide is out as you begin your climb down to Portreath Beach, you should be able to spot Rocky Pool ❼ on the western side of the pier. This tidal bath is said to have been created when an enterprising local 'borrowed' some dynamite from one of the nearby mines and blasted it out of the rocks. A retaining wall keeps the water in, and locals bathe there all through the year. Apparently, the pool was enlarged in 1902, with workers excavating between the tides. It was further enlarged in 1910 to celebrate the coronation of King George V.

Equally impressive are Lady Basset's Baths ❻ on the near side of the beach as you descend. Six bath-shaped pools were carved out on the orders of Francis Basset for his wife Susannah and daughter Frances in the late 18th century. You might also spot the quaint Smugglers Cottage at this end of the beach, used as a retreat by the Bassets, who attempted to create a miniature Brighton in the area, with the pools as one of the attractions. It was believed that bathing in cold saltwater was good for one's health – something that we can attest to with evidence today. It's fun hunting out the baths in the rocks at various heights, with one even found in a cave. The name Portreath comes from the Cornish for 'sandy cove' and, on a calm day, the beach also makes an excellent place to take a dip.

Continuing your walk, you pass under a bridge that once carried the Portreath branch of the Hayle Railway. The horse-drawn tramway was the first railway in Cornwall, and started operating in 1809. Financed by Francis Basset, it carried coal to the copper mines near Scorrier and Poldice Mine near St Day and brought back the ore to the port for onward transportation. On the steeper section of the route, stationary steam winders were used to raise and lower the trucks, with one of these operating on the hillside above Portreath harbour. Today the footpath from Primrose Terrace follows one of the old tramways along part of the Minerals Tramway Heritage Project. This £6 million regeneration project saw 37 miles of paths created for walkers, cyclists and horse-riders along the old mining railway tracks.

The route takes you up through Illogan Woods ⑩, a magical wooded valley, before emerging near the remains of an old mine. When you cross the river or the small stream that feeds it, see if the water is running red. Like several rivers in this part of Cornwall, the flow at Portreath was known as the Red River, due to the minerals from the mines draining into it. You'll then follow 'Tramways' trails to take you into the beautiful Tehidy Country Park ⑫, the former home of the Basset family.

The Basset family lived at Tehidy for more than 700 years, but following the decline in the mining industry sold the estate in 1916. Two years later it became a hospital for tuberculosis sufferers, and it remained a hospital until the 1980s. It was purchased by Cornwall County Council in 1983, and the 250-acre estate was turned into one of Cornwall's four country parks. Today you can enjoy nine miles of paths and trails, a lake, an events field,

outdoor education facilities, a permanent orienteering course and a schools-and-youth campsite. The Bassets' former home has been converted into luxury apartments, which you can see across the golf course.

The walk through the country park is delightful, with ash, oak, beech, sycamore, birch, chestnut and conifers to stroll beneath. In the spring, woodland plants like bluebells, wild garlic and daffodils flower in abundance, while you can also see native ferns and several varieties of rhododendron. Amongst the animals that call the park home are grey squirrels, otters, badgers, swans, geese, rooks and moorhens.

The route back to the car park follows the Pine Walk and Rose Garden, until you reach the North Cliffs Plantation. Here you will find stunted beech trees that have bent away from the south-westerly winds. You might also spot more exotic species including Japanese maples and a monkey-puzzle tree, and in spring the plantation is known for its carpets of bluebells. They all combine to give this area a magical, otherworldly feel that you won't shake off till you are well on your way back home.

1 From Tehidy's North Cliffs car park, walk to the road, turn right and walk 90 metres along the road before turning left onto a track, which leads down to the coast.
0.3 miles

2 Above Basset's Cove, turn right on the coast path, heading north towards Portreath with the sea on your left.
0.5 miles

3 When you reach Carvannel Downs above Porthcadjack Cove, ignore the path to the right, and descend steeply to the valley and up on the far side. Ignoring another path inland to the right, at the top of the hill carry on parallel to the coast above the cliffs until the path returns to the edge.
0.4 miles

4 From Ralph's Cupboard, continue above the beach to approach Western Hill (also known as Treaga Hill). Here you could take the path to the right for a shortcut across the back of the hill, or carry on ahead around the headland, with an optional detour to the top of the hill for breathtaking coastal views.
0.6 miles

5 The two paths reunite above the outermost edge of Portreath. Descend through the houses and down the slipway to the beach for a swim, looking along the rocks to your left for the baths.
0.1 miles

6 From the baths, cross out to the main beach for a proper swim, and then over to the pier to find the tidal pool if the tide is out.
0.2 miles

7 From the tidal Rocky Pool, head up through the beach car park and turn left along the road. Pass the public loos on your right and then take the path down to the right and cross the stream.
0.1 miles

8 By the back garden of the Basset Arms turn left along Tregea Terrace. At the end, opposite the Chinese restaurant, bear right and go under the bridge and along Glenfeadon Terrace and Primrose Terrace.
0.5 miles

9 At the end of Primrose Terrace take a sharp turn to the right and bear right along the footpath to climb steadily through the wooded valley.
0.3 miles

10 The path forks at the head of the valley; take the right fork and continue uphill through the woods and out into farmland. You reach a T-junction of paths and turn right towards farm buildings ahead. Take the path to the right in front of the farm and follow it around the farm and on between fields, then past holiday cottages on the right.
0.5 miles

11 Where the path meets the road, turn left and keep following the path between the golf course and the fields, bearing left before bending right through trees to the road.
0.5 miles

12 Cross the road, going past the car park to into Tehidy Country Park. Follow the path into woodland, keeping the golf course on your left, with the ruins of Tehidy House. There is a choice of routes back to North Cliffs car park; both the pink and blue trails will take you there.
1.3 miles

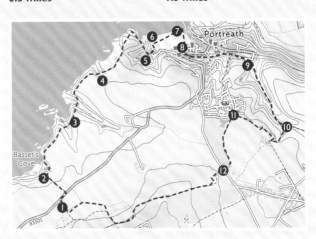

85

Walk 11

ST IVES STEAM AND SWIM

This is a tremendous day out, starting with a spectacular train ride along St Ives Bay, one of the most scenic rail routes in the country. You then walk back, following the coastline, stopping at an array of stunning swim spots.

The day out starts at St Erth station, where you hop on the train for a relaxing ride on what must be one of the prettiest branch lines in England. The journey to St Ives is only 10 minutes long but takes in an extraordinary variety of views, including the Hayle Estuary, Carbis Bay and finally Porthminster Beach. The line first opened in 1877, in the age of steam. At that time St Ives was still a busy fishing port, and a lot of the catch travelled up the line to London. However, tourism was also developing, and many holidaymakers arrived in the resort by train. In the first half of the 20th century, the Cornish Riviera Express ran on summer Saturdays from Paddington to St Ives. In 1968, the notorious Dr Beeching wanted to close the line, but was successfully resisted, and the line is still busy and thriving today.

When you get off the train, if it's the summer season you will be thrust into the hurly burly of St Ives, with its shops, cafés and tourists. It is an attractive town, with many old stone buildings. The author Virginia Woolf stayed here on childhood holidays. Writing in 1939, she described it as "a windy, noisy, fishy, vociferous, narrow-streeted town; the colour of a mussel or limpet; like a bunch of rough shells, oysters or mussels, all crowded together". Enjoy the bustle, knowing you will soon be having a restorative swim: maybe make a diversion up to the Leach Pottery at the top of the town, or spend a tactile hour at the Barbara Hepworth Museum and Sculpture Garden on our route. Make your way through the throng to Porthmeor Beach ❹, the first swim spot, which faces north and is popular with surfers because you normally find big rolling waves here – which are also great fun to jump and body surf in.

INFORMATION

DISTANCE: 7.5 miles
TIME: Allow all day
MAP: OS Explorer 102 Lands End
START POINT: St Erth station (SW 541 357, TR27 6JW), from where the St Ives Bay Line runs twice hourly (timetable at greatscenicrailways.co.uk).
END POINT: St Erth station.
PUBLIC TRANSPORT: Mainline trains from Penzance and Truro serve St Erth
SWIMMING: Porthmeor Beach (SW 515 409), Porthgwidden Beach (SW 521 410), Bamaluz Beach (SW 522 409), the harbour (SW 520 406), Porthminster Beach (SW 522 400), and Porth Kidney Sands (SW 542 386).
PLACES OF INTEREST: Tate St Ives, the Barbara Hepworth Museum, the Leach Pottery.
REFRESHMENTS: St Ives is chock-full of cafés and pubs. The Porthminster Café is right on the beach with spectacular views of the sea, and very popular so you will need to book (01736 795352, TR26 2EB). The Seafood Café has a counter of wet fish from which you make your choice (01736 794004, TR26 1HE).
EASIER ACCESS: All the beaches on the walk apart from Porth Kidney Sands are accessible from the road.
NEARBY SWIM SPOTS: Fishing Cove, just to the east of Godrevy Point, is quiet and idyllic although there is a steep path down and it is used by naturists. Treen Cove or Gurnard's Head Cove is to the west of St Ives near Zennor; it is remote and rocky and best when the tide is out.

The beach is overlooked by the Tate St Ives art gallery, which opened in 1991, in recognition of the town's history as a mecca for artists since Victorian times. Much has been written about the quality of the light in St Ives, with no real conclusions about what makes it so special. But the colour of the sea here really is something to behold, particularly on a sunny day. It's an almost mind-bending experience looking at it and swimming in it, because of the intensity of the blue and the way the light plays in the water and on the fine, white, glitter-like sand.

Walking along Porthmeor Beach heading east, you pass some of the oldest and most famous working artists' studios in the country as part of the terrace of buildings that line the beach. These are the Porthmeor Studios, which started off life as pilchard cellars before the artists came. They have enormous windows, and past tenants here include the painters Ben Nicholson, Patrick Heron and Francis Bacon; they are still used by artists today.

From the eastern end of the beach you head up the slipway and around a tiny headland called The Island. At low tide, look out for a small pool in the rocks, which is surprisingly deep and we call the Mermaid Pool. On top of the island is a chapel that probably dates from the 14th century, although there is no record of when it was built. Dedicated to St Nicholas, the patron saint of sailors, it's been used for worship over the years, but also as a lookout, notably to catch smugglers.

The next swim spot is Porthgwidden Beach ❼ which, in contrast to Porthmeor, is sheltered from the prevailing south westerly winds and usually calm. The sea here is the most stunning turquoise, and incredibly clear, especially if you swim around the rocks to the left side of the beach. There is also an ancient set of stone steps on that side, which you can swim directly off at high tide.

The walk then takes you along the St Ives seafront past Bamaluz Beach ❼. This is bordered on the right by a big stone jetty, which local lads like to jump off, and overlooked by the remains of a tin mine called Wheal Dream. Then there is the harbour beach, right in the middle of town, stuffed full of boats and a place where many people like to stop and watch all the marine activity. After the lifeboat station you reach Porthminster Beach ❽, another spectacular swim spot with acres of white sand as far as the eye can see. It has great views across to Godrevy Lighthouse, the inspiration for Virginia Woolf's novel *To the Lighthouse*.

As it moves away from Porthminster and along the coast path, the walk starts to leave the clamour of the town and feel quieter. You pass an old building called the Baulking House, where you can stop for a sit-down on the sheltered benches and enjoy the views. This is where the so-called 'huers' would look out for the shoals of pilchard. When they spotted a shoal they would raise the alarm (as in 'hue and cry') to let the fishermen know to get their boats out, and direct their chase.

The next beach on the walk is Carbis Bay ❿, another beautiful stretch of glittering sand. It is privately owned but publicly accessible under the Right to Roam. You'll be glad you're on foot, as

the parking is very expensive. It is provided by the exclusive Carbis Bay Estate which describes itself as a 'luxurious coastal retreat', complete with very posh beach lodges and a spa. Luckily it doesn't cost you anything to walk onto the beach!

The walk continues along the coast path around the headland, with stunning views across to the vast dunes of the Towans and a contemporary wooden house high on the clifftop. Just below ⓭ there is a small path off the main path where you can go down to the remains of an old pillbox and swim off the rocks. The sea is stunningly clear here.

The path continues to cling to the coast path, with the railway line alongside. The next beach is Porth Kidney Sands ⓮, which borders the mouth of the Hayle Estuary and is backed by dunes. It feels much wilder than the previous beaches, and at low tide the sand can stretch almost a mile out to sea.

In the final part of the walk, you cross the railway line and a golf course and then pass the ancient Church of St Uny ⓯. Look out for its rather gruesome skeleton sundial. Just outside the church is the starting point of St Michael's Way, a pilgrims' walking route to St Michael's Mount on the south coast and part of a network of trails leading to the shrine of Santiago de Compostela in Spain. The use of this path is thought to date back a thousand years, when pilgrims and missionaries from Ireland and Wales used this route to cross Cornwall to reach the Mount.

The walk then takes you through a very pleasant lane and quiet roads, lined with houses that have lovely gardens, with glimpses of the estuary to your left. After that it's a short trek along a couple of main roads to get back to St Erth station.

DIRECTIONS

❶ There are various ways through the town to Tate St Ives and Porthmeor Beach from the station; this is the route we took. From the station, head out through the car park and past St Ives Travel on the left. Take the steep steps up out of the station car park on the left. At the top of the steps turn right, where immediately on your right is a tremendous viewpoint of St Ives. Follow the road down past the Catholic church on the right and St Ives library on the left.
0.3 miles

❷ At the T-junction turn right opposite Barclays bank. Then turn left by the curved stone building, opposite the Golden Lion pub, into Market Place, and left again at the end. Follow the road uphill as it bends right and on past the Barbara Hepworth Museum on the left, following the brown signs for Tate St Ives up the steep hill.
0.2 miles

❸ At the top turn left and into the car park and follow the path down to Porthmeor Beach, with the Tate gallery to your right.
0.1 miles

❹ On Porthmeor Beach, walk along to the end with the Tate on your right, and up the slipway onto The Island. Follow the path as it hugs the coast around the headland. At the front, as you approach the lookout point, look out for a small pool in the rocks on your left (only around two hours either side of low tide). Walk up to have a look at the chapel.
0.6 miles

❺ From the chapel, walk down to the left edge of Porthgwidden beach.
0.1 miles

6 From Porthgwidden beach, take the steps up at the south end. The path skirts left around the car park and hugs the coast to the next beach.
0.1 miles

7 From Bamaluz Beach, continue to follow the path with the sea on the left. When you reach Smeaton's Pier ahead, turn right and continue to follow the seafront around the harbour beach, down the side of the lifeboat station and on past the station and the headland. If the tide is low enough, you could walk all of this on the sands.
0.6 miles

8 From Porthminster Beach, pick up the path behind the Porthminster Café and follow it as it zig-zags right then left and over a railway bridge.
0.3 miles

9 At a fork by a bench dedicated to Terence John Edwards, bear right. You next reach a crossroads with a path left and a road with double yellow lines right and straight on; take the road straight on. Go uphill along the road past houses including Shun Lee on the right and Wild Air on the left, and the Baulking House with a plaque and its sheltered benches, giving fine views over the whole bay. Carry on through a wood and along a residential road with big houses either side.
0.5 miles

10 You reach a fork where the road goes back into trees – bear left here following the 'Lelant 2.5 miles' sign. Cross the railway bridge and walk uphill for Carbis Bay.
0.3 miles

11 From the centre of Carbis Bay with the sea behind you and the viaduct ahead of you, turn left and follow the coast road uphill for a short distance.
0.1 miles

12 Turn left down the steps at the top, following the coast path sign for Lelant Church as it hugs the clifftop and rounds a headland.
0.4 miles

13 Below the modern wooden house to your right you can do a very short diversion down to a lovely swim spot off the rocks by the remains of an old pillbox. Afterwards rejoin the path and stay on it to the dunes above Porth Kidney, where a short diversion off the coast path leads to the sands.
0.5 mile

14 From Porth Kidney Sands, rejoin the path and walk along it with the railway line on your right.
0.5 miles

15 Cross a footbridge over the railway on your right and follow the path along the edge of the golf course. At a junction with a pillbox ahead saying 'Danger Golf Keep to Path' turn right towards the church.
0.3 miles

16 Just past St Uny/Lelant church you reach a road. Walk ahead along it (do not turn right) for a very short distance. Then, turn left at a grass triangle on the left (this is surprisingly easy to miss). Do not follow the road you are now on straight ahead down to Lelant Beach car park, but immediately bear right by Brookland Court house down a lane, passing a house called Plantation on the right. The lane bends right to run alongside the railway line past Lelant station, then swings inland and continues past houses on the right.
0.9 miles

17 Where the road bends sharply to the right, take a footpath off to the left with fingerpost showing an acorn for the coast path, which emerges into a car park. Turn right and head out of the car park into a street of modern stone houses. At the T-junction at the end turn right, signed for Redruth and Penzance, crossing to the pavement on the opposite side of the road.
0.2 miles

18 At the roundabout follow the path around to the left, also signed Redruth and Penzance.
0.2 miles

19 Just before the large roundabout, cross the road you are on to the path you can see leading away from the road opposite. This skirts past the roundabout to run along the A30 back to St Erth station. Cross the road back to the station, which is on the left.
0.2 miles

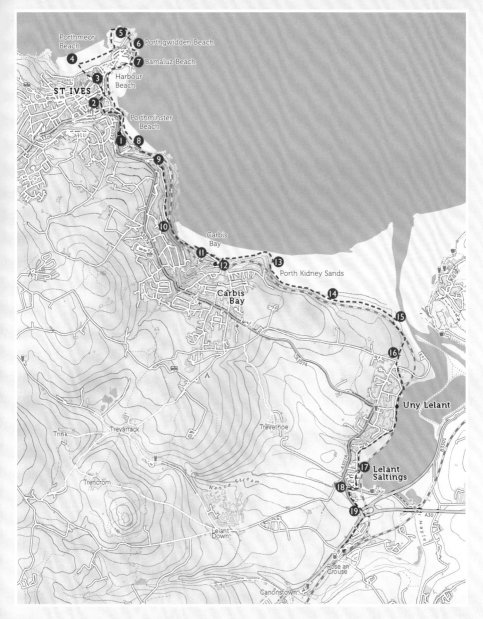

Walk 12

ST JUST CIRCULAR

A breathtaking walk of two coastal valleys and three contrasting beaches, with views to the Brisons, twin islets famous for their annual swim. If you want to visit the tidal pools on the beaches, set out a couple of hours before low tide.

T
he walk starts in St Just, Britain's most westerly town, which is packed with granite buildings giving it a slight Breton feel. The town was once a centre of the Cornish mining industry, and relics of its past are everywhere to be seen in the old chimneys and mine buildings that dot the landscape. This part of the Cornish peninsula feels distinct from the rest of the county. The absence of trees is noticeable, and it truly feels as though you are teetering on the edge of England, surrounded by sea on three sides.

The town is home to one of Cornwall's best known contemporary artists, Kurt Jackson, who has a gallery here. He is mostly known for his large, impressionistic landscape paintings produced 'en plein air' but he also writes and sculpts. He describes his focus as "the complexity, diversity and fragility of the natural world", and has had residencies on a Greenpeace ship, at the Eden Project and at the Glastonbury Festival. His gallery is well worth a visit while you are here.

You leave the town and head down towards Cot Valley ❺, a lush subtropical dell, following a tinkling stream down to the sea. There are a few cottages with flower-filled gardens, and one with the most enormous gunnera plants, and what must be one of the best-situated youth hostels in the country. It describes itself as a 'one-stop location for paradise' and we can't disagree!

The walk emerges at Porth Nanven beach ❹, which locals call Cot beach. It's also known as 'dinosaur egg beach' on account of the smooth, round boulders that lie in profusion at the entrance to the cove. Unfortunately, these have proved rather too attractive to some people, who've taken them to put in their gardens. The

INFORMATION

DISTANCE: 5 miles
TIME: Allow 4–5 hours
MAP: OS Explorer 102 Lands End
START POINT: Car park in St Just
(SW 369 313, TR19 7JB).
END POINT: Car park in St Just
PUBLIC TRANSPORT: Bus route A3
between St Ives and Penzance calls at
St Just. In summer it is open top. Other
buses include the 7, the 8 and the A17.
SWIMMING: Porth Nanven (SW 355
309), Priest's Cove (SW 352 317)
and Porth Ledden (SW 354 321).
PLACES OF INTEREST: Ballowall
Barrow, St Helen's Chapel, Botallack
Tin Mine, The Kurt Jackson
Foundation Gallery.
REFRESHMENTS: The Little Wonder
Café above Priest's Cove at Cape
Cornwall sells hot drinks, delicious
cakes and lots of lovely fare (07980
005885, TR19 7NN). The Café Dog
and Rabbit in St Just is a vegan- and
dog-friendly café (01736 449811,
TR19 7LB). The Star Inn in St Just is
favoured by locals and real ale fans
alike (01736 788767, TR19 7LL).
EASIER ACCESS: Unfortunately, none
of the beaches are easy for people
with limited mobility. You can park
right by Porth Nanven, but have to
clamber over boulders to reach the
beach. At Priest's Cove you can park
nearby, but it is a short walk down to
the cove, although the slipway gives
good access to the water at high tide.
NEARBY SWIM SPOTS: Portheras
Cove is a lovely sandy beach, often
frequented by seals, a short walk
from the village of Pendeen.

95

National Trust, which owns the beach, has had to take measures, and it is now illegal to remove these beautiful stones.

A short distance out to sea are the Brisons, twin islands that locals call 'Charles de Gaulle having his bath' – and they do look very like a rather corpulent gentleman lying on his back having a soak. Why the former president of the French republic and not some other person, distinguished or otherwise, is lost in the mists of time.

The sea here is remarkably clear and blue. There is a huge seaweed forest stretching across the bay and it makes a fascinating swim, especially with a snorkel, as you are likely to see plenty of fish. To the left of the beach at low tide is a stunning natural tidal pool, which locals call the mermaid pool. It is a wonderful place to swim, with calm turquoise waters, and on a sunny day you could be in the Mediterranean. There is another smaller and even more remote beach also to the left, which you can reach at low tide if you're prepared to scramble over the rocks. If you take swim shoes you can spend a happy hour or two exploring here, dipping in the larger rockpools as you go.

After your dip, the coast path takes you along towards the next swim spot, but there is an interesting ancient monument you can take a short diversion to see on the way. Just before the Carn Gloose headland ❻ is a path to the right signed for the Ballowal Barrow. This is an unusually complex tomb combining Neolithic and Bronze Age elements, which historians believe was sited at the top of the cliffs in order to provide a dramatic and striking shrine. The barrow was excavated in 1878 by the Cornish antiquarian William Copeland Borlase. It contains a number of stone box structures, called cists, in which urns of human ashes were found.

The next swim stop is Priest's Cove ❼, which is overlooked by Cape Cornwall, topped by a chimney stack which is over 150 years old and was retained as a daymark after it fell out of use for Cape Cornwall Mine. There were scores of tin and copper mines in this small area of Cornwall, with some of them even extending out to sea, which transformed the landscape in the 18th and 19th centuries. The area is part of a UNESCO World Heritage Site in recognition of the international significance of its mining history.

As you walk down towards Priest's Cove you will notice a grand house on the skyline to the right. This was built in 1909 by Francis Oats, a local mine captain who went out to seek his fortune in the diamond mines of South Africa, and came back as chairman of the De Beers diamond mining company to build a home. You can see the remains of his concrete beach hut – complete with staircase – at the back of the beach.

Priests's Cove has a small fishing fleet of colourful boats. You may also see a fleet of brightly painted Land Rovers, which they use to haul the boats up the slipway. There is a tidal pool believed to have been built in the 1920s. A local swimmer, Ros Luxford, has an amazing story about it: in 1967, aged eight, she was being taught to swim there by her dad, who lost his wedding ring in the pool. Despite great efforts, it could not be found, and that was that. So imagine her surprise when, 49 years later, in 2016, the ring was discovered during a clear-out of the pool – not only that, but her father just happened to be visiting the cove that very day.

The cove is also home to the annual Cape sports day, the highlight of which is the Brisons Swim, which has been going for years. It usually takes place in August, depending on tides and conditions, and involves participants being taken out to the islands by boat, and then swimming the mile back. Ros did the swim to celebrate her 60th birthday, and says it

you at the other end). At low water, you can cross the beach on foot, picking your way over the boulders, which come in a huge variety of shapes, sizes and colours, and swim at the northern end. There's a wonderful rock platform at this end, where you can swim in various intriguing gullies and pools.

From the beach, you follow the path up along the tiny Tregeseal river, a beautiful little stream with the odd waterfall, up the Kenidjack valley. This little watercourse powered the various mining operations in the area, evidence of which is still visible today. You pass the extensive remains of the Kenidjack Arsenic Works, part of the Carn Praunter Tin Mine. These works extracted arsenic from the tin, which was otherwise virtually unsaleable.

was very exciting. "It was like being inside a washing machine in the sea," she says. I looked behind me and the Brisons looked like mountains. "I really enjoyed the challenge."

After a dip at Priest's Cove, you head for the next beach. On the way is a diminutive ruin on the headland, St Helen's Chapel ❽, the remains of a medieval oratory with an ancient weathered cross on one gable end. Beyond it a path leads down to Porth Ledden ❾, ending in a rather rickety slipway that was used by local fishermen up until the 1960s. This beach is popular with seals, who can often be seen 'bottling' just offshore. This is when they rest or sleep upright, with their heads out of the water.

If you want to swim here, it depends on the tide, but you do need to end up at the northern end of the beach in order to follow the route back to St Just. If it's high, you can dip off the slipway at the southern end but then you'll have to take the path back and over the cliffs (unless of course you want to swim across of course – you'll need to carry your stuff in a waterproof bag or get a friend to carry it and meet

A short way after this you can divert left onto the coast path ❿ for half a mile to visit Botallack Mine. One of the most famous mine ruins in Cornwall, and featured in the TV series *Poldark*, it produced thousands of tons of tin, copper and arsenic. Its workings reached half a mile out to sea, and it became a tourist attraction even in the 19th century, following a visit by the Prince and Princess of Wales in 1865. The mine decided to cash in by charging visitors a guinea for the privilege of a short mine tour! After your free visit, retrace your steps and continue uphill.

At the top of the valley you reach a handsome bridge over the river ⓬, which you cross before heading over the fields and back into St Just, emerging by its historic church ⓭. It's worth a look inside for the ancient carved stone pieces, and the unusual and rather primitive looking medieval frescoes; one shows Christ with the tools of his trade including a compass and a scythe, and the other St George fighting a not-very-threatening dragon. After that there are plenty of cafés and hostelries for a well-earned rest and refreshment.

❶ Turn left out of the car park main entrance and left again at the T-junction, walking past the playground on your right. Pass the Methodist Free Church on your right, and then go past another playground on your right.
0.3 miles

❷ You reach a junction with a no-through-road sign ahead where the road you are on bends left. Head down the dead end lane, walking past houses, and at the end turn right onto the public footpath.
0.4 miles

❸ At the youth hostel sign turn left. Just past Brook Cottage turn right at another youth hostel sign to cross the stream, go past Daisy Cottage on your left and then the remains of an old mine on your left. Turn right to cross the stream and then left into the road. Stay on the road – do not take the coast path sign to the right. Follow it down, cross the stream to the left and head down to the beach.
0.6 miles

❹ From Porth Nanven, retrace your steps inland up the road about 350 metres and take the little path up to the left just past a concrete layby on the right, where there is a sign saying 'National Trust mine shafts'. You can see the handrail halfway up the path and a house at the top.
0.3 miles

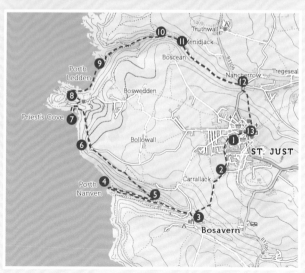

❺ At the top of the path is a T-junction with signs for the coast path and Ballowal. Turn left here and keep on the path. Only take

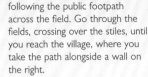

the turn for Ballowal monument if you want to make the diversion, and return to the coast path after.
0.6 miles

6 You reach Carn Gloose headland. From here follow the road to the left and then take the track left down to Priest's Cove.
0.3 miles

7 From Priest's Cove, walk back up a little and take the stone steps to the left up to the road. Turn right and then take the first left through a metal gate with a National Trust sign into the field with the ruined chapel.
0.2 miles

8 From St Helen's Chapel go straight on and through a metal gate, then turn right to walk down to the beach. If it is low tide you can walk across. If it is high, you will need to retrace your steps to the road where you entered the chapel field, turn left, and then follow the coast path left below Porthledden House along to the northern access to Porth Ledden beach.
0.4 miles

9 From the north end of Porth Ledden beach, walk up the valley following the stream on your right. Keep going towards the old mine and continue as the path leads onto a lane.
0.5 miles

10 You reach a coast path sign to your left. Here you can divert and walk north to see Botallack Mine (adds another mile onto the distance), then retrace your

steps to this point and carry on up the valley.
0.2 miles

11 There is a sign for 'Poldark Eggs 'on your left and a bridge on your right. Carry straight on along the lane here.
0.5 miles

12 At a crossroads with the Tregeseal Gallery opposite, cross the bridge to the right and then in 40 metres turn left off the road up the steps by the St Just sign,

following the public footpath across the field. Go through the fields, crossing over the stiles, until you reach the village, where you take the path alongside a wall on the right.
0.3 miles

13 You emerge by the church, turn right and head into the main square. Walk past the Wellington Hotel on your left and take the second left, Market Street, back to the car park which you will find on your left.
0.1 miles

Walk 13

PORTHGWARRA AND NANJIZAL CIRCULAR

An exhilarating stomp around some of the most dramatic coastal scenery in Cornwall, taking in a magical sea cave with a natural arch and pool, known as the Song of the Sea. This walk is best done around low tide.

INFORMATION

DISTANCE: 4.5 miles
TIME: Allow 5 hours
MAP: OS Explorer 102 Lands End
START POINT: Car park in Porthgwarra (SW 371 218, TR19 6JP).
END POINT: Car park in Porthgwarra.
PUBLIC TRANSPORT: None.
SWIMMING: Porthgwarra Cove (SW 371 216), Nanjizal (SW 357 236).
PLACES OF INTEREST: Porthgwarra Tunnel and hulleys, Funnel Hole, Song of the Sea.
REFRESHMENTS: Porthgwarra Cove Café is open most of the year apart from November – January (01736 871754, TR19 6JB). The Apple Tree Café in Trevescan roasts its own coffee and is dog-friendly (01736 872753, TR19 7AQ).
EASIER ACCESS: It is a short walk to Porthgwarra Cove from the car park. Unfortunately, Nanjizal is not easy for those who are less mobile, because of the boulders. However, there is a shorter walk to Nanjizal if you park in Trevescan and make your way from there.
NEARBY SWIM SPOTS: Porthcurno is a spectacular beach with easy access from a large car park; Whitesand Bay at Sennen Cove is great for surfing.

The walk starts in the tiny hamlet of Porthgwarra ❶, with its well-kept stone cottages and a rather wonderful café with a lovely garden. It's part of St Aubyn Estates – 5,000 acres of land in West Cornwall owned by the St Aubyn family, who live in the castle at nearby St Michael's Mount. The cottages can be hired out for holidays. Time your walk to start about an hour before low tide, because the sea cave and pool at Nanjizal disappear about two hours after low water, as the sea fills them up and covers them.

The crystal waters of Porthgwarra featured in several scenes in the latest TV adaption of *Poldark*, most notably when Ross stripped off for a swim there. It has an intriguing tunnel down to the beach, which you mustn't miss. Before you set off on the walk, head to the left of the slipway, past the house festooned with buoys. Shortly on the right you will find the tunnel, carved out of the rock and helpfully lined on both sides with rope banisters.

The tunnel was made in the late 19th century, when fishing was still a big industry in the village. It improved access to the beach, in particular so fishermen could get to shellfish storage tanks that they created in the rocks. You can still see these 'hulleys', as they're called, at low tide, by going through a second archway on the left-hand side of the beach, to the rocky part of the cove. They are listed as monuments by Historic England because of their rarity. The fishermen created them using the granite blocks already on the beach, and stored their shellfish catches there, keeping them alive in the seawater until they were ready to be sold. Apparently, the tanks even had specially made wooden lids.

Porthgwarra is a lovely place for a swim; there are usually seals around, so look out for them and if you see them keep your distance. If you're starting the walk around low tide it's better to wait and swim here at the end of the walk, when there will be more water.

The walk takes you up onto the monumental, tor-like cliffs, which look like buttresses jutting out to sea. One member of the party on a recent trip described it as 'Dartmoor on Sea'. The Victorian novelist Wilkie Collins wrote about this part of the coast in a highly entertaining account of a hiking trip to Cornwall in 1850, called *Rambles Beyond Railways*: "It's granite, and granite alone that appears everywhere – granite… presenting an appearance of adamantine solidity and strength, a mighty breadth of outline and an unbroken vastness of extent nobly adapted to the purpose of protecting the shores of Cornwall, where they are most exposed to the fury of the Atlantic waves."

There are various paths along the coastline; if you're not comfortable with heights, keep to those further away from the cliffs. If you're happy to go along nearer the edge, you get to the Funnel Hole ❷, a large blowhole which gave this headland its original name. In Cornish it is Tol-Pedn-Penwith, which means 'the holed headland in Penwith', although it's now better known as Gwennap Head. Look out for choughs, a once-rare Cornish bird which is black with orange legs and beak; we saw one fly up out of the blowhole, squawking indignantly at being disturbed.

As you walk you will notice two strange-looking cones; they are to aid shipping and mark the Runnel Stone, a hazardous rock pinnacle about a mile off Gwennap Head. Apparently, as long as mariners can see the black-and-white one they're fine; however if the red one obscures the black-

and-white one they could be in trouble, as that means they're very near the pinnacle.

You pass the National Coastwatch Institution ❸, where volunteer coastguards keep watch over this section of Cornish waters, which has been the demise of many ships over the years. The headland is a great place to sport marine wildlife, notably dolphins and other cetaceans, as well as a huge variety of seabirds. One of the team at the Coastwatch is a naturalist and publishes regular fascinating reports of her sightings on their website. In January 2020 alone she saw common dolphins, harbour porpoises, bottlenose dolphins, a Minke whale and even a rare pilot whale.

The walk takes you down to Nanjizal (pronounced Nanjizzle) Bay, which is also known as Mill Bay ❹. There is a wooden staircase leading down to the beach, which is littered with large boulders. The beach is very changeable; sometimes there is a lot of sand, sometimes none at all. The natural arch is on the left-hand side, and can be a challenge to get to as you have to clamber over the boulders. But the effort is worth it, as you are rewarded with the most magical blue inlet, dominated by an elegant arch, a narrow slit like the eye of a needle.

Its name is Zawn Pyg in Cornish, but it is also known as Song of the Sea and, not surprisingly, has been painted and photographed by countless artists. There is even an early black-and-white photograph of it from the 1860s in the John Paul Getty collection, which you can see online. It's best visited in the afternoon, at low tide, when there's more chance of the sun shining on the water, but if you can visit in the afternoon in December and January you may get the chance to see a rare natural phenomenon: the sun setting through the arch. At this time of year the winter sunset aligns with the viewpoint through the arch, giving it a beautiful glow. However, your swim might be a tad chilly at that time of year!

Saying that, swimming in the pool – whatever the season – feels like being in a fairy tale. The graceful arch looms above, and the water is turquoise because of the white sand. It varies in depth according to the amount of sand and the state of the tide, but it always feels like a very special place to be.

After your dip, the walk heads inland for a short while, going via two farms which are medieval in origin: Bosistow ❻ and Ardensawah ❼. Take care not to get lost around Bosistow; the paths are confusing and not well marked. Once you get to Ardensawah, the walk is straightforward again, taking you back to the heathland that borders the coast. This area is an SSSI, as many migrating birds pass through including guillemots, shearwaters, razorbills and fulmars. There are also many other native birds to see including linnets, stonechats, wheatears and shrikes.

It's a flat and then downhill walk back to Porthgwarra, where you can have a final swim before settling down to a much-deserved cream tea in the café.

DIRECTIONS

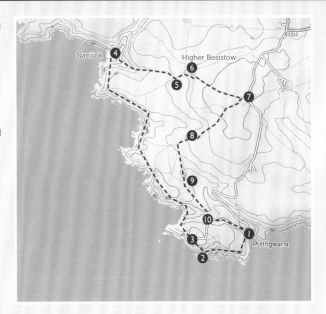

1 From the car park either head to the beach for a dip or save it for later, then follow the coast path for Lands End. Stay on the path following the cliff edge to Gwennap Head.
0.4 miles

2 You reach the blowhole called the Funnel Hole. Keep walking along the coast path.
0.1 miles

3 From the National Coastwatch building, continue along the headland hugging the coast before eventually heading down toward a beach where you see a large house on your right, via the steps by the wooden bridge over the stream.
1.5 miles

4 On Nanjizal beach, climb over rocks to find the Song of the Sea on your left. From the beach, go back to the coast path via the wooden bridge. Turn right and head straight on up the hill in a south-easterly direction. The path becomes a track and meets with the driveway from the house on the cliff. Pass through a granite gate and over a granite cattle grid. Continue between fields, through a second metal gate and then through a wooden gate next to a metal gate.
0.5 miles

5 Turn left, and then shortly right at the next junction of paths where you can see buildings ahead.
0.1 miles

6 Opposite Bosistow Farmhouse, turn right over the granite stile/steps and follow the left border of the field. Turn left through the gate and cut diagonally across the next field, following the track towards the gateway. Continue diagonally across the next field, heading towards the farm, and when you reach it follow the path around to the right.
0.4 miles

7 Turn right away from Ardensawah Farmhouse, following the sign for 'Three Chimneys to Coast Path'. You are now heading south-west towards the coast. Continue past St Aubyn Estate cottages.
0.4 miles

8 Go through the gate that says 'Welcome to RSPB Porthgwarra'. Continue straight(ish) about 300 metres, and at the fork head left towards the Coastwatch station. Keep bearing left at forks, so that you are heading towards the daymarks at the back of the common.
0.3 miles

9 At the pond, keep to the right-hand side of it and continue straight.
0.3 miles

10 Turn left onto the lane, go past a house on your right and continue back to the car park. Head down to the beach for a well-earned swim.
0.3 miles

Walk 14

PERRANUTHNOE AND PRUSSIA COVE CIRCULAR

A walk around a notorious stretch of smugglers
coastline, along a series of beautiful coves and
swim spots, all with enigmatic names and
intriguing stories behind them.

T oday's adventure starts at the beach at the small village
of Perranuthnoe, a somewhat difficult to pronounce
name which comes from Piran, the patron saint of
Cornwall, and Uthno, the local manor. The beach
itself has the much easier name of Perran Sands ❷. It's best to start
during the lower half of the tide, to enjoy the numerous tidal pools
and gulleys on offer. The walk is set in the amazing surroundings
of Mount's Bay, with the world-famous tidal island of St Michael's
Mount to the west. The bay is famous for its clear turquoise waters
and dramatic rocky coastline.

You can have a refreshing dip at Perran Sands before setting off
along the coast path, which takes you off to the left of the beach
and on towards Trevean Cove ❹. The cove can be reached through
a gully that was once a slipway used by fishermen to haul their
boats off the beach at high tide. Trevean is the name of a nearby
hamlet and comes from the Cornish words 'tre' meaning settlement
and 'vean' meaning small. While you can swim from the beach, it's
much more fun to explore the rocky outcrops off to the left, which
are of great interest to geologists for what they tell us about the last
ice age, when Mount's Bay was dry land. We were more attracted to
the pools and gullies that you can swim in at low tide. The flat rocks
are great for sunbathing, and we also found a fantastic jumping spot,
although do obviously check the depth first.

Continuing on along the coast path, you will next spot even more
swimming temptations down at Stackhouse Cove ❺ with its flat
rocks and natural pools. The cove was named after marine biologist
John Stackhouse, who lived at nearby Acton Castle during the
18th century. He carried out detailed studies of the seaweed on the

INFORMATION

DISTANCE: 4 miles
TIME: Allow 6 hours
MAP: OS Explorer 102 Land's End
START POINT: Car park in
Perranuthnoe (SW 540 294, TR20
9NE), parking attendant and toilets.
END POINT: Car park in Perranuthnoe
PUBLIC TRANSPORT: Bus routes
including the U4 from Falmouth,
A17/39A from St Ives, 39A from
Penzance and 46/U1/U4 from Truro
stop near the beach in Perranuthnoe.
SWIMMING: Perranuthnoe/Perran
Sands (SW 539 292), from the rocks
near Trevean Cove (SW 544 287),
Stackhouse Cove (SW 549 282),
Bessy's Cove (SW 557 279).
PLACES OF INTEREST: Stackhouse
Cove baths, Cudden Point, Little Cudden,
Bessy's Cove tracks, St Michael's Mount.
REFRESHMENTS: The Cabin Beach
Café is just above Perran Sands and sells
homemade cakes and scones and freshly
ground fairtrade coffee (01736 711733,
TR20 9NE). The Peppercorn Café is in
the Lynfield Craft Centre in Perranuthoe
(01736 719584, TR20 9NE).
EASIER ACCESS: Perran Sands is a
short walk from the car park, with easy
access. The only parking for Prussia
Cove is a small private field car park -
busy in summer. It's a five-minute walk
and scramble down to the beach.
NEARBY SWIM SPOTS: The National
Trust-owned Rinsey Cove, or Porthcew,
between Praa Sands and Porthleven, is
beautiful and dramatic, and has a natural
tidal pool in the rocks. Marazion beach
is a safe swim spot with St Michael's
Mount as a spectacular backdrop.

beach, which he published in 1797 in an illustrated book with the catchy title of *Nereis Britannica; or a Botanical Description of British Marine Plants, in Latin and English, accompanied with Drawings from Nature.* His findings remain the widest range of seaweed species ever recorded in Great Britain in one place, so don't forget your goggles if you go for a dip here. He built the castle for his wife Susannah in the belief that the sea air would be a tonic for her poor health. He also had two baths cut into the rocks for her to bathe in, believing that the seawater and seaweed also had curative properties. And who are we to disagree? One is on the beach and a second is in a cave, where spring water keeps it topped up. If you are hunting for it, look for a narrow oval opening with green algae growing from where the freshwater seeps out.

Soon you will climb up to Cudden Point ❻, a rugged headland with a rocky spine resembling the back of a prehistoric monster. According to legend, an incredible bounty lies hidden on the seabed beneath the headland, waiting to make someone rich beyond their wildest dreams. In the 19th century, children would come from across the county to search the sands on a spring tide, when much of the seabed was exposed. The treasures waiting to be discovered apparently include gold coins, jewellery and silver goblets, although the ultimate prize is a huge table made of solid silver.

In the story, a wealthy cad invited a party of his equally wicked friends on a sailing party around Mounts Bay. They dropped anchor off Cudden Point, where they drank and feasted around the silver table. However, even though it was fine weather, the boat and all of their riches sank into the depths for no discernible reason. For years later, old fishermen would say they heard the sound of laughter and the clinking of goblets coming up from the watery deeps. Some would say that when the sea was calm and clear, they could see the guests seated around the table on the seabed still partying with the fishes. But they would tell you any tale for a drink…

The views from here are simply magnificent, and it's a perfect spot for a picnic. It is believed that the point, now managed by the National Trust, may have been an Iron Age cliff castle. On either side of the headland are two 'zawns,' which are chasms or inlets in the cliff – on the east is Zawn Harry and on the west is Zawn Susan, next to Western Shag Rock. The small building above the headland was a coastal observation station in the First World War. As you bear around the point, you will pass through a gap in the wall marked by a pair of wooden posts, into which people have pressed coins.

The next small headland is called Little Cudden, where you can see what seems to be the remains of an old chapel. A curious plaque says 'We have a building of God, a house not made with hands, eternal in the heavens; where the spirit of the Lord is there is liberty'. There is also a wooden pole with a hole and chains, one of the moorings for HMS Warspite left as a memorial. The Queen Elizabeth class battleship was built in Devonport docks in 1912 and took part in the Battle of Jutland, the largest naval battle of the First World War. She also saw service throughout the Second World War, before being sold for scrap in 1947. While underway to the breakers, she ran aground at Prussia Cove. She was later refloated and towed to Mount's Bay to be broken up.

Ahead of you lies a series of coves and beaches that make up an area known as Prussia Cove – first Piskies Cove ❼ then Bessy's Cove ❽ and finally King's Cove (the cove most people call Prussia Cove 'proper'). The name comes from the

Carters, a notorious family of local 'freetraders', who smuggled illegal cargoes ranging from rum to tea into the bay in the 18th century. Their leader John Carter gained the nickname 'King of Prussia' in childhood games he played with his brothers. The name stuck, and the area was informally renamed in his honour, although the Cornish name remains Porth Legh (Slab Cove). The cove we will be swimming at is called Bessy's Cove after Bessie Bussow; she ran the Kiddleywink Inn, which once stood above the cove. A 'wink' was an unlicensed alehouse, and legend says a tunnel from the inn to the beach below kept the hostelry amply stocked with rum, tobacco and other exotic contraband.

By the tumbledown granite fishing huts, you can walk down a steep track to one half of the cove, which resembles a natural harbour. A copper mine once operated from the cove and coal was landed here, and later it was used by a fishing fleet; evidence of this industry, including a rusting winch, can still be seen. The slabs of rocks off to the right make a wonderful swimming spot, with pools, caves and swim-throughs to be explored. The area is also popular with divers and snorkellers, and conger eels, pollack and trigger fish are all to be spotted in the area. You can see across to the small shingle beach that makes up the other half of Bessy's Cove from here, which can be reached from a path a little further on. Looking down between the two sections of the cove there are cart tracks cut into the rock, which were used for hauling up seaweed to be used as fertiliser.

The cove really is a magical place to swim, while you let your mind drift back to its smuggling past. We swam off to the left of the beach, where you will find rocky lagoons to explore and rocks to sunbathe on. You will be able to spot the charming thatched Cliff Cottage above, which dates back to the time

of the smugglers and once operated as an unofficial tavern with its own distillery. Later used as a guesthouse, today it operates both as holiday accommodation and as a filming location. In 2001, Charles Dance used the house and gardens as the setting for his *Ladies in Lavender*, starring Judi Dench, Maggie Smith and Miriam Margoyles, and the cove itself was used in the original *Poldark* back in the 1970s.

Following your swim stop, the return journey takes you up past Cliff Cottage and onto a lane, before crossing over fields and through farm buildings. It's a very attractive route with views back to St Michael's Mount. This striking tidal island with a castle and chapel is linked to the town of Marazion by a man-made causeway. Owned by the St Aubyn family from around 1650, the island today belongs to the National Trust, while the family still live in the castle. Two round-the-island charity swims take place each year. It's a fairly challenging mile and a half, taking in amazing views of the island and the bay, with a pasty waiting for you at the end.

The walk finishes back in Perranuthnoe. If you are in need of some refreshment, why not pop into the Victoria Inn, which dates back to the 12th century and is one of the oldest recorded inns in Cornwall; it has no doubt served a smuggler or two in its past.

DIRECTIONS

1 From the car park walk down the hill to Perran Sands for a swim.
0.1 miles

2 From Perran Sands, retrace your steps back towards the car park and turn right at the coast path sign saying 'Prussia Cove 2m'. Stay on the coast path, keeping right at the postbox, and keep following it.
0.7 miles

3 You reach a fork where you bear right to keep following the path close to the coast.
0.1 miles

4 As you round the end of the headland, take a path to the right which leads you down to Trevean Cove. Once on the rocky beach, head left where there are pools and swim-throughs across the rocks at low tide. Afterwards, rejoin the coast path and keep heading south-east.
0.2 miles

5 You reach a stile on a bend, where there is another opportunity to walk down to the sea for a swim from the rocks of Stackhouse Cove, rejoining the path after. Cross the stream over the railway sleepers and then pass the sign saying 'National Trust Cudden Point'.
0.5 miles

6 Walk up the steep hill over Cudden Point and past a pair of posts bearing a coast path acorn emblem and with coins pressed into them. Continue over the headland until you can see the first of the three beaches that make up Prussia Cove.
0.2 miles

❼ Follow around Piskies Cove, keeping right if the path ever splits. When you reach some old, low fishermen's buildings on your left, one thatched, a right turn will take you down the slipway.
0.3 miles

❽ At a low-ish tide in Bessy's Cove you can walk around the rocks to the right to find various pools and even a small swim-through. Afterwards, head back up to the coast path, turning right away from the buildings. Continue up the hill past the postbox and bear left at the fork, then follow the stony track around and uphill inland.
0.2 miles

❾ By the car park turn right onto the lane, then follow the lane around to the left and on for a couple of minutes.
0.2 miles

❿ Look for a public footpath sign on your left, right next to a wooden gate. Go over the stile and follow the left edge of the field. You will spot another stile in the middle of the far hedge, to the right of the houses. Cross over this and follow the left edge of the next field around the corner and on into another field, before exiting through the wooden gate in the corner onto the lane.
0.4 miles

⓫ Turn right onto the lane. Stay on the lane, ignoring the footpath sign on your left.
0.1 miles

⓬ Turn left through Trevean Farm, and then turn right around

Beare's Den campsite. Follow the left-hand edge of the field, ignoring the stile in the corner on the left, and instead cross the stile halfway along the top edge of the field. Follow the right-hand edge of the next field, passing through a wooden kissing gate at the end.
0.4 miles

⓭ Walk past the converted buildings at Trebarvah Barn, bearing slightly left to cross the gravel car

park, and then bear right onto the path at the public footpath sign. Follow the path along the right-hand side of the field and stay on it back to the village.
0.4 miles

⓮ The path emerges in the village main road opposite the Victoria Inn. Turn left and walk back along the road to the car park, which you will find on the left.
0.1 miles

115

Walk 15

MULLION FIGURE OF EIGHT

A looping walk on the dramatic Lizard Peninsula, with a charming harbour swim featuring rock islands, smugglers caves and mysterious tunnels to explore.

INFORMATION

DISTANCE: 6.5 miles
TIME: Allow six hours with swims and lunch
MAP: OS Explorer 103 The Lizard
START POINT: Poldhu Cove car park (SW 667 199, TR12 7JB); you cannot pay by card, so bring change.
END POINT: Poldhu Cove car park
PUBLIC TRANSPORT: Bus route L1 from Truro serves Mullion and Poldhu.
SWIMMING: Polurrian Cove (SW 667 187), Mullion Cove (SW 666 178), Poldhu Cove (SW 664 199).
PLACES OF INTEREST: Marconi Centre, The Lizard National Nature Reserve, Predannack Cross.
REFRESHMENTS: The Poldhu Beach Café does takeaway light bites and amazing hot chocolates, as well as their own range of clothing (01326 240530, TR12 7JB). Glenbervie Bar at the Mullion Cove Hotel offers drinks, informal food and Cornish cream teas with a dog-friendly lounge (01326 240328, TR12 7EP).
EASIER ACCESS: Access to Poldhu Cove from the car park is fairly flat and sandy. There is a car park at Mullion Cove and it's a 5-minute walk down the road.
NEARBY SWIM SPOTS: Gunwalloe Beach, also known as Church Cove (1 mile round walk from Poldhu Cove) is a pretty place to swim and was featured in *Poldark*. Kynance Cove is a legendarily beautiful swim spot that has inspired poets, painters and wild swimmers; it can get very crowded though, so go at low water when there is more beach.

Today's walk starts at Poldhu Cove ❶, on the east side of Mount's Bay, before heading south along the coast via Polurrian and Mullion Coves and then back inland. Poldhu is Cornish for 'black pool', which couldn't be any further from the truth. This is actually a lovely golden sandy beach, albeit very popular with locals and 'emmets' alike. We then head up over the cliff towards the imposing building that was formerly the Poldhu Hotel, built in 1899 and now a care home.

Sherlock Holmes and Dr. Watson stay in a cottage overlooking Poldhu Cove in *The Adventure of the Devil's Foot*, the only one of Sir Arthur Conan Doyle's sleuthing adventures set in Cornwall. In the spring of 1897, Sherlock is sent to convalesce on the Lizard peninsula on his doctor's advice, but his supposedly relaxing holiday walking and studying the Cornish language is, of course, interrupted when a baffling mystery presents itself. The views from the headland back down towards the cove are stunning (especially in bluebell season), although Watson clearly isn't in a holiday mood when he describes them: "From the windows of our little white-washed house, which stood high up on a grassy headland, we looked down upon the whole sinister semi-circle of Mounts Bay, that old deathtrap of sailing vessels, with its fringe of black cliffs and surge-swept reefs on which innumerable seamen have met their end."

Another famous person to stop over on the headland was Guglielmo Marconi, who stayed in the former Poldhu Hotel in May and August 1901. He was there to oversee the building of the Poldhu wireless station, which went on to transmit the first transatlantic radio message on 12 December 1901. Marconi received the transmission himself on Signal Hill, St John's,

Newfoundland. The station closed and was later demolished in the 1930s, but you will pass a stone monument pillar that was erected in November 1937 by the Marconi Company in honour of the remarkable achievement.

The Marconi Centre ⑭ opened on the headland in 2001, exactly 100 years to the day after the first transmission. The museum is owned and maintained by the National Trust and is run by volunteers from Poldhu Amateur Radio Club. It's free to enter and includes a short film, short-wave radios to listen to and a self-guided tour of the adjoining fields, where the ruins of the old transmitter can be seen. Children can also get a certificate for tapping out their name in Morse code.

The walk then crosses Angrouse Cliff before dropping down to Polurrian Cove ❸, a sandy beach backed by high cliffs. At low water, the beach extends for over 300 metres, although there is still about half that on a high tide. The sea off this south-west-facing beach is often quite boisterous, so be careful swimming there if this is the case. However, on a calm day you can swim around the rocky headland of Polbream Point off to the right, jumping from the rocks along the way. Off to the right-hand side of the rocky outcrop in the middle of the beach is another fun area to explore called Sandy Pedn-y-ke. The cove also marks the geological boundary between the Cornish slates and granite of Mount's Bay and the rare ocean crust rocks of the Lizard, pushed up by a collision of two ancient continents millions of years ago.

The walk heads up a steep path to pass the Chocolate Factory and Craft Centre on the road between Mullion village and Mullion Cove. It's worth pausing to browse the various businesses, which include craft shops, art galleries, a glass studio, a stationery and gift store and a coffee shop. Most importantly, you must stop to say hello to some very friendly llamas in the field behind the car park. The walk then heads back onto a footpath and across fields with lovely views over the bay to your right.

You pass an area called Ghost Hill on your left, which surrounds an old copper mine called Wheal Unity or sometimes Ghost Croft Mine. The spooky name comes from the boggy land where copper ore was first discovered in the 1720s. Apparently, gas released from the marshy ground would spontaneously glow, creating a phenomenon called will-o'-the-wisps. You can imagine it would be terrifying if you were walking across the boggy fields and found yourself accompanied by flashing, floating lights. It's definitely worth wearing a stout pair of walking boots on this stretch of the walk, just in case.

As you continue, the walk starts to feel much more moor-like as you enter the Lizard National Nature Reserve. This stretches from Mullion Cove in the west, across Goonhilly Downs in the centre of the peninsula, to Lowland Point near Coverack in the east. It is famous for rare plants including dwarf rush, wild asparagus and Cornish heath. Along the route you will pass Predannack Cross ❽ on your left, a wayside cross that served the dual purpose of reinforcing the Christian faith amongst those who passed it while also acting as a waymarker. Crosses like this were erected from the 9th to the 15th century, and there are around 400 of them in Cornwall.

The path then passes between cottages before joining a track past some old quarries and down towards the coast, where you will have expansive views from the rocky outcrop on Mullion Cliff, out over Mullion Island. The more romantic amongst our party compared it to Kirrin Island from the *Famous Five* books, the more humorously inclined see a phallic resemblance. It's a great place to look out for choughs, peregrines and ravens soaring above the steep cliffs, while the heathland smells of camomile as you continue the stunning walk over the headland back towards Mullion Cove ❾. Hundreds of boats have met a watery end along this stretch of coast, which is why local landowner Lord Robartes built the harbour in the 1890s, as a safe haven for local fishermen.

After pausing to photograph the cove, where youngsters will inevitably be jumping from the harbour walls on a high tide, it's a steep walk down to the 19th-century harbour. The name Mullion probably comes from the Cornish 'Porth Mellin', which means Mill Cove and describes an old mill that once operated here. Historically the harbour was also home to a small pilchard fleet, and an old pilchard cellar remains on the quayside, together with the historic lifeboat station. The harbour is still used today by a few fishermen who set out pots for crab and lobster. The National Trust owns and maintains it, which is good news, as the fierce Atlantic regularly batters the piers.

There's a small sandy beach here at low tide and on a calm day it's a great place to swim from. Swimming out of the harbour walls to the right, you can circumnavigate a rock island called The Var, which only appears on a falling tide. Further adventures await you off to the left. If you swim along the outside of the southern harbour wall, back towards the shore, you will see a small beach called Porth Pyg, by a cave. A second smaller cave on the left contains a tunnel stretching right back through the southern cliff to the harbour. Known as Torchlight Cave since Victorian times, it has been used to store smuggled contraband.

In her 1884 book, *An Unsentimental Journey through Cornwall*, novelist Dinah Maria Craik describes the cave in the most sentimental of ways:

"The most exquisite little nook, where you could have imagined a mermaid came daily to comb her hair. What a charming dressing room she would have, shut in on three sides by those great walls of serpentine, and in front the glittering sea, rolling in upon a floor of silver sand." It's an amazing scramble back to the harbour following the light ahead, as the amplified sound of the water splashes and echoes through the passageway.

Perhaps following some refreshments from the small shop, the walk then climbs out of the harbour up a steep path to the rather posh – but dog friendly – Mullion Hotel and Spa. You'll pass a cannon that was found in the harbour when the walls were being built, as well as a lookout and bench called Love Rock. Unfortunately, there isn't some sweeping story of tragic star-crossed lovers behind the name, but a simple mistranslation of the Cornish name Carrag Luz; while 'carrag' does indeed mean rock, 'luz' actually means grey. Grey Rock doesn't sound quite so romantic, but nothing can diminish the magnificent views across Mount's Bay to Penzance.

The walk then heads up the valley from Polurrian Cove and through a field near Angrouse Farm ⓭ where John Wesley, the father of the Methodist movement, preached in 1762. A stone in the field says 'ST 1762' with the ST referring to Samuel Triggs, the owner of the farm, who invited him to preach. A plaque in the corner of the field tells the story in more detail. Incidentally, 'grouse' is Cornish for cross, and the name might mean that another medieval wayside cross once stood here. The walk finishes by walking around the far side of the Marconi Centre ⓮ and back down towards the beach and the car park where we started. Why not reward yourself with one final swim before the drive home? You'll have earned it.

1 From the car park next to Poldhu Cove beach, head towards the public loos on the left-hand side of the beach. Follow the road to the left of the loos towards the nursing home.
0.3 miles

2 By the footpath left to the Marconi Centre, take the small footpath to the right down the steps, following the small metal coast path sign with the acorn. Follow the coast path, keeping as close to the sea on your right as you can, around the headland and down to the beach.
0.9 mile

3 At Polurrian Cove stop for a swim, then continue south along the coast path up a steep incline.
0.3 miles

4 The path emerges at houses and the Polurrian hotel. Do not turn right along the coast path where it says private road, or left, but continue straight ahead into the road. Pass properties Berrow and Polurrian Cottage on your left, and a street called Gwel-an-Garrek on your right.
0.1 miles

5 Just past Gwel-an-Garrek turn right down Trenance Lane. At the end of the lane, you reach a road. Cross over and walk down the lane with the dead-end sign. Pass a green public footpath sign on your left.
0.3 miles

6 Shortly after the footpath sign on the left, there is one on the right. Turn right here, crossing a slate stile, and follow the path over a few fields and stiles.
0.2 miles

7 You emerge onto a track with a granite post to the left. Cross to go straight on over a stone stile, following the footpath through fields, wilder land, and fields again, passing Predannack Cross before seeing a house beyond the last field.
0.7 miles

8 After the white-and-stone house on the left, turn right along a track, passing Mount View on the left. Follow the path past Pradanack

Morva and Gull Rock Cabin on the left, towards the coast and Mullion Island ahead (ignore the track on the right here). Follow the path at the coast as it bears right, with the sea on your left.
1 mile

9 At Mullion Cove swim and explore, then walk back up the slipway and turn left up the stone steps to the left of Island View, following the small metal coast path sign. Follow the coast path past the Mullion Cove Hotel on your right, keeping to the left of the National Trust 'Polurrian Cliff' sign. You pass Love Rock on the left before arriving back at point 4 where you turn left to retrace your steps for a short distance.
0.8 miles

10 You reach a fork in the paths above Polurrian Cove beach. Take the right-hand path signed 'Polurrian via slope'. You reach a T-junction of paths and turn right, then ignore a small path forking to the left after 40 metres, and keep going. The path bends left and crosses a stream and then a field.
0.3 miles

11 You reach a T-junction and turn right, then shortly another junction of paths and tracks. Keep going in the same direction here, past a bungalow on your right then Mulberry Cottage and Mere on the left.
0.2 miles

12 At a fork with a postbox on the right, turn left following the yellow arrow and the home-made

'Footpath' sign. Pass through some granite posts, following the yellow arrow to the left. Cross a field with houses on the right and the sea on the left. Cross a stile, a boardwalk and then another field.
0.3 miles

13 Cross the stile with a stone plaque referring to John Wesley and turn left onto the track. Follow the track as it passes Angrouse Farm House and Wireless Waves on the left, turns left past Seven Pines on the right, and makes more bends out to the headland.
0.6 miles

14 At the Marconi Centre turn right by the gate that says 'Welcome to the Marconi Centre' onto the road. Turn right and follow the road back to the car park.
0.4 miles

Walk 16

POLTESCO AND CADGWITH CIRCULAR

This walk incorporates some beguiling aspects of Cornwall's history, from a historic coastal serpentine quarry to a working fishing village, along with an unusual swim into a collapsed cave known as the Devil's Frying Pan.

INFORMATION

DISTANCE: 3 miles
TIME: Allow 3 hours
MAP: OS Explorer 103 The Lizard
START POINT: Car park in Ruan. Minor (SW 719 153, TR12 7LE).
END POINT: Car park in Ruan Minor.
PUBLIC TRANSPORT: Bus route 34 from Lizard, Helston and Redruth.
SWIMMING: Carleon Cove (SW 728 156), Little Cove, Cadgwith (SW 722 144).
PLACES OF INTEREST: Poltesco Barn, Carleon Cove, Cadgwith.
REFRESHMENTS: Ruan Minor Store has a great café (01326 290138, TR12 7JL). The Cadgwith Cove Inn is the perfect half way stop-off point (01326 290513, TR12 7JX).
EASIER ACCESS: There is a small car park at Poltesco Barn, from where it is a short walk down to Carleon Cove. For Cadgwith, park in the village car park and walk down to the beach.
NEARBY SWIM SPOTS: Housel Bay is a small cove with dramatic cliffs either side, best swum at high tide. Kennack Sands is also fun, especially for children, with a long expanse of sand and rockpools to explore.

The walk starts inland in Ruan Minor ❶, which has one of the best village shops we've found. The store, which also has a post office, sells pretty much anything you might need, including posh takeaway salads, and the wooden seats and tables outside are a lovely place to sit in the sun and enjoy a coffee.

Setting off from the car park, which is in the middle of some modern housing, you pass the school and then descend a curving lane past a pretty thatched white cottage. You cross the bubbling Poltesco stream, full of moss-covered boulders and cascades, and then pass a house with one of those bizarrely memorable plaques saying 'On this site, September 5th 1782, nothing happened'.

The beach and much of the valley are owned by the National Trust, and at this point on the walk it is interesting to stop off at Poltesco Barn ❸, where an exhibition sets out the history of the place. You can listen to stories from the past, and also see some fascinating artefacts including ancient slingshots.

After the exhibition, the walk leads you down over an unusual wooden bridge ❹, designed by a local architect, Matt Robinson. It was built in 2013, after the previous one came to the end of its natural life, out of oak, larch and fir with stainless steel rigging, and looks like an exaggerated version of the clam bridges you find on Dartmoor.

You then emerge onto what must be one of the most unusual beaches in Cornwall, Carleon Cove ❺. Stone ruins crowd the left-hand side of the cove, and the stream spreads out and becomes a large pond behind the shoreline. The buildings are the remains of 17th-century pilchard cellars and a 19th-century serpentine quarry. Pilchard fishing was big business in the 1600s, with scores of boats heading out to sea with large nets, in which thousands of fish were caught. They would be brought ashore in baskets and sorted and graded in the fish cellars before being sent off to be sold. The round building on the beach is the remains of the Capstan House, which contained a large winch used to drag the boats up the beach.

The pilchard industry went into decline in the 19th century, but by this point the cove had a new use as a quarry. Serpentine, found in quantities on the Lizard, is a distinctive red or green stone, used to make ornamental pieces including fireplaces, vases and gravestones. The Lizard Serpentine Company was formed in 1853; Prince Albert was its most famous customer, buying pieces for the royal home on the Isle of Wight. The company repurposed the old pilchard cellars, and times were busy on the beach for the next 30 or so years.

Novelist Dinah Maria Craik describes a visit to the quarry in her 1884 book *An Unsentimental Journey through Cornwall*: "The monotonous hum of its machinery mingled oddly with the murmur of a trout stream which ran through the pretty little valley, crossed by a wooden bridge, where a solitary angler stood fishing in imperturbable content. There were only about a dozen workmen visible … very delicate and beautiful was the workmanship; the forms of some of the things – vases and candlesticks especially – were quite Pompeian … we should have like to carry off a cart-load – especially two enormous vases and a chimney piece – but travellers have limits to luggage, and purse as well."

The beach is a beautiful place for a swim, and the sea very clear because of the preponderance of pebbles and lack of sand. You can even rinse off afterwards with a dip in the pond behind the beach, if there's enough water in it. During the autumn and winter months when the stream becomes full, the pond is quite large, and you can lie in it looking out to sea; it feels like an infinity pool.

The next part of the walk takes you along the coast path, with dramatic sea vistas. You walk towards Cadgwith ❻, with lovely views down to the village's twin coves, one containing several fishing boats. This is one of the last small fishing communities in Cornwall. In the centre of the village is a single plank bench against the wall of one of the buildings. The writer C.C. Vyvyan, who was a friend of Daphne du Maurier, describes how this bench was known as 'the stick', where the older fishermen used to settle like 'snails in a wall' and put the world to rights. It's a good place to stop and have a rest and watch the activity around the boats.

Swimming at Cadgwith is extremely pleasurable, with plenty of interest. Don't swim from the harbour cove but the one next to it, which is called Little Cove ❼. The two are separated by a rock outcrop called the Todden, which the youth like to jump off, as is their wont. There's also a channel through the Todden when the tide is high enough, which is fun to swim through.

The Devil's Frying Pan, around the corner to the right from Little Cove, is an enclosed pool that you swim to under a rock bridge. It is actually a collapsed sea cave, and a swim to it is a wonderful adventure. It gets its name because when the sea fills it in stormy weather, it looks as though the water is boiling. You used to be able to see this dramatic pool from the coast path, but sadly there has been a cliff fall and the path has been diverted away – the photo here was taken before the cliff fall. Swimming to the Devil's Frying Pan is easily now the best way of experiencing it.

The swim is not far, about 300 metres, but should only be attempted when the sea is flat and there is no wind. It is best done in the top half of the tide, and the best time to start swimming is at slack water, an hour before high tide. Swim out along the right-hand side of Little Beach. When you get to the opening of the cove, turn right and head south, hugging the coast on your right. After a short while you will see a channel, which goes under a dramatic rock arch like a bridge and opens out into a large lagoon. It is thrilling swimming under the natural arch and into the pool.

The walk takes you back into the village and along a path that passes several picturesque cottages and then a corrugated iron building, known as the blue tin church, erected in 1895. This is actually the local St Mary's Anglican church. There is a notice on the wall stating proudly that electric light was installed in the church after the Second World War, in thanks for the fact that the village was spared from enemy action.

After a look round the church, which usually has an array of second-hand books for sale, you walk inland and back to Ruan Minor, where virtually the first building in the village you see is the shop – ideally placed for a refreshing cuppa.

DIRECTIONS

1 Turn right out of the car park, right again at the T-junction and follow the pavement past the village hall.
0.1 miles

2 Cross the road and turn left just before the school. Ignore the footpath sign and continue past the churchyard on your right. Follow the lane and wind down the lane, eventually crossing a bridge.
0.5 miles

3 Turn right in front of Poltesco House and then turn right before the 'Discover Poltesco' National Trust display at Poltesco Barn. Cross the wooden bridge and follow the footpath signed to Carleon Cove.
0.1 miles

4 Head left at the fork and down steps to cross over an unusual curved wooden bridge, continuing down onto the beach.
0.1 miles

5 After a swim at Carleon Cove, retrace your steps over the bridge and then turn left at the fork. Follow the coast path around the headland, before it eventually turns down into Cadgwith as a lane, bearing left down into the village.
1 mile

6 Walk past the harbour with its boats on your left and continue uphill. At the top bear left and down to find Little Cove.
0.1 miles

7 From Little Cove, go back to the village and start back downhill towards the first beach.
0.1 miles

8 Turn left before the thatched cottage, following a sign that says 'Footpath to car park'. Walk past the small wooden chapel and continue up the path towards the village car park.
0.1 miles

9 When you reach the stone stile, do not enter the car park. Instead take a slight right following the 'Woodland Walk' path. At the pumping station, take the right-hand fork until you reach a road.
0.3 miles

10 Turn right onto the road, crossing the stream. Go straight on at the bend on the road, following the public footpath sign and then the sign for Trelowarth. Turn right at the waymarker. Follow the path back to the village, emerging onto a lane with Ruan Minor Methodist Church on the left.
0.3 miles

11 Turn left onto the road after the church, then left at the post office and village store onto the footpath. Walk past the toilets on the right and turn left onto the road. Turn left down the footpath beside the village hall (on the far side), which leads back to the car park.
0.1 miles

Walk 17

FRENCHMAN'S CREEK CIRCULAR

Take a gentle walk through one of the most dreamily romantic parts of Cornwall. For swimming opportunities, the walk is best done around high tide.

INFORMATION

DISTANCE: 3 miles
TIME: 3 hours
MAP: OS Explorer 103 The Lizard
START POINT: Helford village car park (SW 759 261, TR12 6JU).
END POINT: Helford village car park.
PUBLIC TRANSPORT: Bus route 323 from Falmouth, Perranporth, Truro, Bodmin and Penzance.
SWIMMING: Penarvon Cove (SW 756 263) and Frenchman's Creek (SW 747 262).
PLACES OF INTEREST: Helford, Chapel of St Francis of Assisi, Kestle Barton.
REFRESHMENTS: Kestle Barton has a small tea hut with an honesty box system (01326 231811, TR12 6HU). The Shipwrights Arms makes a perfect refreshment stop for thirsty wild swimmers, with impressive views of the river (01326 231235, TR12 6JX).
EASIER ACCESS: Penarvon Cove is a fairly accessible stroll from the car park involving footpaths and small hills. If you park at Kestle Barton, Frenchman's Creek is a short walk downhill on a rough track.
NEARBY SWIM SPOTS: Take the ferry across to Helford Passage and the Ferryboat Inn. You can swim 1 mile downstream to Durgan Beach and take the coast path back. There are also lovely swim spots on the Helford side of the estuary, including Bosahan and Ponsence Coves.

*F*renchman's Creek will always be inextricably linked with Daphne du Maurier's novel of the same name. Set during the reign of Charles II, it tells the tale of a headstrong English lady and a French pirate, and du Maurier said it was "the only one of my novels I am prepared to admit is romantic". In her pictorial memoir *Daphne du Maurier's Enchanted Cornwall*, she explained the reason for writing a romantic novel set in this picturesque flooded valley: she sailed up the Helford River and into Frenchman's Creek for her honeymoon with husband Tommy Browning. "We couldn't have chosen anything more beautiful," she reminisced. Her memories of this magical and enchanting place are shared through the evocative descriptions in her novel: "...there, suddenly before her for the first time, was the creek, still and soundless, shrouded by the trees, hidden from the eyes of men. She stared at it in wonder, for she had no knowledge of its existence, this stealthy branch of the parent river creeping into her own property, so sheltered, so concealed by the woods themselves... The creek twisted around a belt of trees, and she began to walk along the bank, happy, fascinated, forgetting her mission, for this discovery was a pleasure quite unexpected, this creek was a source of enchantment, a new escape... a place to drowse and sleep, a lotus-land."

The walk begins by dropping down into the pretty village of Helford ❷, where a medieval settlement was first recorded in 1230, and crossing the stream over the wooden bridge. On the far side are attractive cottages with whitewashed walls, many of which are former boathouses and fish cellars. You'll pass Helford Village Stores, an ideal place to pick up supplies, and the tempting sight

of the Shipwrights Arms, which you can visit at the end of your adventures. There are splendid views across the Helford River and on down towards its mouth. In the summer months (Easter through to October) a small pedestrian ferry, which has been operating since the Middle Ages, can take you across to Helford Passage in around 10 minutes.

The walk then continues up over a small headland before dropping down to Penarvon Cove ❹, which is a great little secret beach for a swim, sheltered from the wind and with trees providing some lovely shade in the summer months. Aim to arrive around high tide, because as the waters retreat, they leave a shingle shoreline and mudflats. It's a really pretty spot with colourful small boats in various states of repair towards the back of the beach, and everything overlooked by the charming Penarvon Cottage, which a sign informs you is where boat launch fees can be paid.

Before continuing, it is possible to take a small diversion (half a mile) by turning right at Penarvon Cottage, following the sign for Pengwedhen Woodland Walk. Pengwedhen means 'head of the fair stream' in Cornish, and in the summer the area is carpeted with wildflowers. The woodland is owned by the National Trust and also contains the tiny chapel of St Francis of Assisi, the patron saint of animals. At the end of the path you will discover a small shingle beach at low tide. Return to the cove to follow the route signposted to Frenchman's Creek, turning left at the cottage and up the hill. You will be rewarded with spectacular views across the Helford when you get to the top.

In early spring these fields are filled with daffodils, adding vibrant colour to the walk. As you turn left at the entrance to Frenchman's Creek ❺, you will be able to see Polwheveral Creek bending away from the Helford at what is known as Groyne Point. If you take a detour following the 'Creekside' path (which eventually comes to a dead end at the mouth of the creek), you will find an old boat buried in the mud, and some steps down to the river, which is another nice swim spot. You might also see egrets, which are like small herons with white plumage and yellow legs.

According to the book *The Artist Who Loved Boats*, the boat was called the Iron Duke and owned by sailor, artist and adventurer, Percy 'Powder' Thurburn. After an adventurous youth, he moored up here with his wife Ann in 1919 or 1920 and they decided they wanted to live on what was then an area of gorse, bracken and scrub called The Downs. They first rented and later bought the land, building a wooden house where they lived a simple life with no telephone, gas or electricity. He planted daffodils, violets, primroses, honeysuckle and yellow gorse in the garden, and pine and eucalyptus trees to shelter them from the north wind. About 20 years before his death in 1961 he donated the house, gardens and some surrounding land to the National Trust. Today you can rent the property, which is called Powders. It includes a private quay that would make a perfect spot to swim from.

Returning to the main path and dropping down close to the creek on your right, it's a matter of finding a safe place to swim and to get out again. We found a spot near an old tree that had fallen in the water and made a natural climbing frame. On a high tide, it's fun to cross the brackish water to the other side, feeling like you have conquered a new land. It's easy to see why Daphne du Maurier was enchanted by the area, as there really is something mysterious and timeless about this quiet and dreamy creek. "As the solitary yachtsman creeps forward the creek narrows, the trees crown

also a small tea hut where you can help yourself using an honesty box. We'd highly recommend a glass of apple juice made from their own apples. Any profits go into funding their arts programme, which includes four free exhibitions in the gallery each year, as well as talks, workshops and other events. They are open to visitors from April till late October.

The descriptions of Navron House in *Frenchman's Creek* sound as if du Maurier may very well have based it on the mansion that once stood at Kestle Barton. Indeed, she describes many features of the old house that were reused in the farmyard barns. These include a 16th-century fireplace and two pillars that once formed the entrance to the house; according to a historic building analysis these can be found in the walls of the buildings of Kestle Barton today. The name Navron is also very similar to the name of Penarvon Cove, which we walked past earlier.

yet more thickly to the water's edge, and he feels a spell upon him, fascinating, strange, a thing of queer excitement not fully understood."

There are various theories about why this stretch of water is known as Frenchman's Creek. Could a French person have lived on the shores in the past, or could it have been named after a French ship that may have used these waters for anchorage? Or perhaps Daphne du Maurier wasn't far off the mark and the waterway was named after a French pirate or smuggler. The truth has been lost in the sands of time, but it still remains an alluring name.

At the end of the path where the creek begins to narrow, head up the hill where daffodils, primroses, violets and wild garlic carpet the woodland floors in the spring. You'll soon enter the yard at Kestle Barton ❽, which is well worth a stop. This ancient Cornish farmstead today boasts stunning holiday accommodation, as well as an elegant gallery, gardens, wildflower meadow and orchard. There's

From the yard at Kestle Barton, you go through a gate in a field and follow the path down into Under Wood. A bridge ❾ carries you over the same stream you crossed at the start in Helford, and it's then a pleasant walk through the woods and along a muddy track back into Helford village. Here you should really indulge in some refreshment at the Shipwrights Arms, a charming thatched pub that dates back to the 17th century. Inside, nautical knick-knacks give the place a traditional feel, including some rather saucy figureheads and fascinating artwork. Outside, terraces drop down to the river, where the views are incredible, especially at high tide. It's the perfect place to sit back and let your mind drift off with a pint of Cornish ale and some fish straight from the Helford River. Is that a pirate boat you can see, stealthily making its way up towards Frenchman's Creek?

DIRECTIONS

1 From the car park, turn right and follow the road down into the village.
0.1 miles

2 Cross the stream on the wooden footbridge and turn right, with the water on your right. Pass the shop on the left and the Shipwrights Arms on your right.
0.2 miles

3 Just after the pub turn left uphill, and halfway up the hill turn right following the public footpath sign. Follow the path to the water, and bear left to the head of the cove.
0.1 miles

4 From Penarvon Cove, you can take a short diversion into Pengwedhen Woodland if you wish, then return and follow the sign for Frenchman's Creek inland from Penarvon Cottage.
0.2 miles

5 At the top of the lane turn right and walk along the left-hand side of the field. At the end of the field on your left there is a gateway; turn left on the track here.
0.3 miles

6 Turn left at the sign for Frenchman's Creek and walk through the woodland. After a short distance you can make a short dead-end detour off to the right, where a sign says 'Creekside', which takes you to the mouth of the creek where you can see the Iron Duke wreck. Return to the main path and walk

with the creek on your right, looking for a spot to swim.
0.6 miles

7 As you get to the top of the creek follow the path to the left and uphill, and then the track as it bends around to the right of a house with a big stone in front of it and on to the road.
0.3 miles

8 Cross the road and past Kestle Barton art gallery on the right. Follow the track ahead to go through a gate into a field, walking along the left-hand side of the field.
0.3 miles

9 At the end of the field go through a gate into the woods, and follow the path down to cross the stream. Follow the path,

with the stream on your left, back down into Helford.
0.2 miles

10 Divert over the wooden footbridge for refreshment at the Shipwrights Arms, or take the road back up to the car park.
0.1 miles

Walk 18

MABE QUARRY CIRCULAR

A pleasant amble through an ancient parish little-visited by tourists, following old quarrymen's routes through farmland to a hidden quarry with a magical, dark pool. It is best done when the weather is dry, as the paths can get very muddy.

INFORMATION

DISTANCE: 3 miles
TIME: Allow 2–3 hours
MAP: The walk straddles OS Explorers 105 Falmouth and 103 Lizard; OS Landranger 204 Truro and Falmouth does cover the whole area.
START POINT: St Laudus church car park (SW 757 325, TR10 9JG).
END POINT: St Laudus church car park.
PUBLIC TRANSPORT: None.
SWIMMING: Spargo Downs Quarry (SW 750 332).
PLACES OF INTEREST: St Laudus' Church, Spargo Downs Quarry.
REFRESHMENTS: Nothing on the walk itself, so take supplies; there are lots of eateries in nearby Penryn and Falmouth. Muddy Beach, on the waterfront in Penryn, is fun and friendly (01326 374424, TR10 8FG). The Wheelhouse Crab and Oyster Bar in Falmouth is very popular so book ahead (01326 318050, TR11 3DQ).
EASIER ACCESS: It is a relatively easy 0.8-mile walk to the quarry from the church car park, first on the road and then on a rough track with a slight incline. You can then go back the way you came to the car park.
NEARBY SWIM SPOTS: Porth Navas Creek on the northern side of the Helford River is a fun swim at high tide. Maenporth beach is a lovely place for a swim too, with a nice café.

The walk starts by the granite church of St Laudus ❶, with its square tower topped by four typical Cornish 'bunny ears'. The origins of the building go back to the 15th century; most of it was destroyed and rebuilt when it was hit by lightning in 1866, not that you can tell. The church is often shut but it's well worth having a wander around the churchyard; there is a medieval wayside cross just to the south of the building, and a prehistoric standing stone under a yew tree.

There are many beautiful gravestones, adorned with lichen, several bearing the unusual surname Spargo, which is also the name of the two hamlets north-east and south-west of the church, Lower and Higher Spargo. The Spargo family has a long history in the parish, and includes John Spargo, the first biographer of Karl Marx, who left Cornwall and emigrated to the United States. It is still quite a common surname in the county.

The parish of Mabe is very close to one of Cornwall's biggest conurbations, Falmouth and Penryn, yet feels a world away. It is home to some medieval farmsteads including Trenoweth (from the Cornish 'tre' meaning settlement and 'noweth' meaning new), which was first recorded in 1314. Its history goes back even further, with records on old maps of Iron Age settlements, known as rounds. These were farms set in stone circular ramparts, but their remains were mostly obliterated when quarrying started in the area in the 18th century.

The village is on Carnmenellis granite, a section of Cornwall's rock 'spine' formed around 300 million years ago. In the 18th and 19th centuries the greatest concentration of the Carnmenellis

Sacred
TO
THE
Memory
OF
THOMAS SPARGO
Who Departed this Life,
The 9th of March 1855,
Aged 72 Years.
Also of
ELIZABETH SPARGO
DAUGHTER OF THE ABOVE
Died 18th of Decr 1859,
Aged 22 Years.
Also of
NICHOLAS SPARGO,
SON OF THE ABOVE
who departed this life,
on the 10th of Decr 1844,
Aged 28 Years.
Also JANE, wife of the above
THOMAS SPARGO.

granite quarries was in this area. Colin Bristow, an expert on the quarrying of Cornish granite, says by 1840 at least 40 quarries were marked on the tithe map for Mabe parish. The stone was excavated and taken by horse-drawn wagons to the nearby port of Penryn, with a six-strong team of horses able to pull 12 tons of granite. The route was so familiar to the horses that, apparently, they didn't even need a man to drive them! From Penryn, it was sent all over the country for building projects as diverse as Waterloo Bridge and Chatham dockyard.

A short distance along the road from the church, you turn left past a complex of old buildings with a rounded end. This farm built of granite dates back to Tudor times, and in the 19th century it served as the poorhouse. You head up a green lane, past a flower farm run by florists who grow a sumptuous range of blooms including dahlias, daisies, lupins and lilies. This lane is one of many footpaths in the parish that were originally the quarrymen's routes to work.

At the end of the green lane, you turn left and follow the path as it winds through a thicket of tall hawthorn and blackthorn bushes. They are absolutely covered in silvery green lichen, which is a sign the air is really clean. You might glimpse water down below to your left, but it is, unfortunately, inaccessible. Go a little further, and turn right at the dead end, and suddenly you come across a high-sided pool, a forgotten and abandoned quarry ❹.

This is known locally as Spargo Downs Quarry. It seems to have been owned by a Scotsman called George McLeod, who came to Cornwall to seek his fortune in 1913. He hooked up with a pair of locals, Richard and Joseph Richards, who owned several quarries. According to the *London Gazette* of 1915, the business relationship was 'dissolved by mutual consent', but leaving MacLeod with this quarry. George McLeod then went into partnership with the local quarrying firm, Freeman's, and was still a director at his death in 1953; the company finally closed its doors in 1965.

The quarry is very inviting, with smooth, dark water, mossy boulders around the side, and rather forbidding grey walls. Swathes of ivy drape from the stone, and the walk to it through the sometimes-prickly vegetation recalls to mind the fairytale of *Sleeping Beauty*, where the prince must make his way to her through a forest of trees, brambles and thorns. There is an atmosphere of hidden mystery as you swim in the cool, clear water, feeling secluded from the outside world, occasionally accompanied by electric-blue damselflies.

After your swim, the walk takes you out of the quarry area, past old concrete posts that are more signs of its industrial history. You pass through fields and cross an ancient granite stile and clapper bridge over a stream – pretty much every built structure on this walk is made of granite. You come out by another old farmstead, Goodagrane Farm ⓭, and follow a track with the remains of old quarries all around you. Three are owned by an adventure charity, which offers outbound activities including canoeing and abseiling, and even has a zipwire!

This area through which you are now walking has an intriguing secret history. Near to the track is an area called Little Palestine, which was home to a secret operational base of the British resistance in the Second World War.

In 1940-41 the country stood alone against Nazi Germany and faced the real possibility of invasion. The government came up with a plan for a secret British resistance, involving local cells of guerrilla fighters, blandly named auxiliary units. The history of Britain's 'secret army' has only come to light in the last 30 years and its existence is still not officially recognised by the Ministry of Defence.

The idea was that if the Germans invaded, a secret network of civilian saboteurs would attack them from behind their own lines, targeting aircraft bases, railway lines and depots, as well as assassinating senior German officers. They were even trained to kill British collaborators, and also locals who might have seen what they were up to. Each unit consisted of between four and eight men, often farmers or landowners with intimate knowledge of their local areas, who would be able to hide in the day and then operate at night under cover of darkness.

They set up operational bases, or OBs as they were known, where they could hide. The Mabe unit was under the control of Lieutenant Alec McLeod – the son of George McLeod. Their OB was in a local quarry, with the bunker built into

the side of the spoil heap. There is a fascinating account on the British Resistance Archive website, detailing how the men dug out the base in the side of the heap, and lined it with timber. They were equipped with knives, pistols and horseshoe-shaped magnets with which to attach explosives to railway lines. Members of the patrol referred to themselves as 'Churchill's favourites' but also as the 'suicide squad'.

Mark Kessell, who used to run the village pub, remembers a conversation in the bar between two elderly men in the 1980s, which went along the following lines:

"Well Frank, you was in the secret army, I knawed you waas. But what good would you have been able to do, if Jerry really had invaded?" Frank had heard this many times over the years, and clearly had had enough from this particular chap.

"Well, Dick! The first thing I myself would have been detailed to do is this... 'cos you and your mum and dad lived on Boscrannock Farm and our ammunition hide was built into a hedge at the bottom of your four-acre meadow, my orders would have been to take the three of 'ee OUT! You would not have had such a clean death if Jerry had got hold of 'ee!"

Dick turned pale as a clout. He realised that Frank had not been joking!

The walk continues past another quarry pool, Trevone Quarry, which you can glimpse to your left. Tantalisingly, it is obviously used for leisure purposes as there are various canoes visible, but it is privately owned and therefore off limits. This area is home to various small businesses including a forge and a rum distillery. The walk continues along a lane past several properties, including one with a rather spectacular treehouse, and re-emerges onto the lane and back to the church.

DIRECTIONS

❶ From the church car park, turn right and walk along the road until you reach the hamlet of Lower Spargo.
0.2 miles

❷ Just before Rosswithian Holiday Lets (a barn with a curving end), turn left up a track. Go past a gate with 'Naturally Green Countryside Services' on it and the field for Rose Valley Farm Flowers, and keep along the track past a stone stile, until you reach a path T-junction.
0.5 miles

❸ At the T-junction turn left. Follow the path, ignoring the first turn on your right and water glimpses on your left. Follow it down until it peters out, and turn right at the end to find the quarry.
0.2 miles

❹ From Spargo Downs quarry, retrace your steps and take the first left, which is the path you ignored on the way in. The path has concrete posts alongside.
0.2 miles

❺ You reach a T-junction of paths. Turn left towards the entrance to a farm.
0.1 miles

❻ You arrive at a track, opposite a farm called Carnebo; turn left onto the track.
0.2 miles

❼ Where the track peters out after a bend, bear right down a grassy path.
0.1 mile

❽ You arrive at a riding school exercise ring. Turn left here by the granite triangle.
0.1 miles

❾ Cross a stone stile and clapper bridge over a stream, then shortly after that cross a stone stile to the left and go through a wooden gate into a field, crossing diagonally to the opposite corner.
0.2 miles

❿ Go through a five-bar gate with 'Please close' on it, then through a seven-bar metal gate.
0.1 miles

⓫ Shortly after, you reach a crossroads of footpaths, with stepped stone stiles in the walls either side of you – note that these are very easy to miss! Take the left stile and follow the edge of the field, with the hedge on your left. Note the wind turbine to the right.
0.1 miles

⓬ At the end of the field is another stone stile to climb up and across to the next field. Keep walking in the same direction, but now with the hedge on your right. At the end of the fields you keep going in the same direction on a track.
0.2 miles

⓭ At the end of the track, by some farm buildings, are stone steps in a wall on the right. Climb up these and over the wall, going past a house called Garden Studio on your right.
0.1 miles

⓮ Coming out of Garden Studio, turn right up the track, opposite the gate with Goodagrane Farm on it.
0.1 miles

⓯ The track bends to the right, with a path on the left. Turn left down the path.
0.1 miles

⓰ The path emerges onto a track, with a building called The Forge on the left. Follow the track all the way back to the road, going past a sign for alpacas on the left, an unusual tree/summerhouse on the right, and bearing left past an old stone trough.
0.5 miles

⓱ Joining the main road at a T-junction on a bend, turn left and follow the road back to the church.
0.3 miles

Walk 19

TRELISSICK FIGURE OF EIGHT

A proper swim safari exploring the creeks off the River Fal and the extensive wilds of the Trelissick estate, with ample swimming opportunities along the way.

Today's walk starts from the car park at Trelissick ❶ heading south down the hill with glorious views over Channals Creek and out towards the River Fal. You'll soon arrive at a shingle beach in front of a remarkable slate wall ❷, where a swim ahead of today's adventure is highly recommended. We swam from the far-left side of the beach, just by the steps built into the wall. As you enter the jade-coloured waters, the view stretches for miles past harbours and wooded banks on towards Falmouth. Directly opposite is Turnaware Point, which was one of the embarkation points for the D Day landings. Understandably, the area attracts a wide range of birdlife, including grey herons, kingfishers and little egrets, as well as a variety of ducks including mallard, teal and shelduck.

The water was clear and refreshing and as we turned back towards the shore, the views up towards Trelissick House were impressive. Originally a farm, the site passed through a succession of owners, including the mining family of Thomas 'Guinea-a-minute' Daniell, reputed to be the richest man in Cornwall. The house you see today was built in the 18th century, with additions made throughout the 19th century. Other owners included Viscount Falmouth of Tregothnan and the Copelands, who were the owners of the Spode china company and gave the house to the National Trust in the 1950s.

Once dried off, continue along the 'South Woodland Walk', which follows the curve of the creek onto the main river, with glimpses of the inviting blue waters through gaps in the twisted oaks. In the woods we also spotted beech, ash, hazel and yews. There is a real *Swallows and Amazons* feel to this stretch of the

INFORMATION

DISTANCE: 4.8 miles
TIME: A good 4–5 hours with swims.
MAP: OS Explorer 105 Falmouth & Mevagissey
START POINT: National Trust car park at Trelissick (SW 836 396, TR3 6QL), free to members, advance book.
END POINT: National Trust car park at Trelissick.
PUBLIC TRANSPORT: Truro station is 5 miles, and bus route 493 runs from Truro to Feock via Trelissick. There are ferries from Falmouth, Truro and St Mawes in the summer.
SWIMMING: Trelissick beach (SW 836 391), South Woods (SW 838 387), Lamouth Creek (SW 834 400, SW 835 402 and SW 837 403) and Roundwood Quay (SW 839 403).
PLACES OF INTEREST: Trelissick house and gardens, King Harry Ferry, various Normandy landings. embarkation points, Roundwood Quay.
REFRESHMENTS: Crofters Café at Trelissick itself (National Trust) is at the start and finish of the walk (01872 862090, TR3 6QL). Linden Hey Tearoom in Feock to sample locally grown Tregothnan teas and delicious cakes too (01872 865106, TR3 6QU).
EASIER ACCESS: Limited free parking on the lane down to Roundwood Quay, the slipway and steps (caution, can be slippery).
NEARBY SWIM SPOTS: Loe beach near Pill Creek is picturesque and swimming is great on a high tide. Swanpool Beach near Falmouth is a lovely sandy beach that backs on to Swanpool Lake Nature Reserve SSSI.

walk and a tempting swim spot can be reached by scrambling down to a small beach below ❸. The path continues past an oyster farm, which is the last remaining oyster fishery in Europe still to be dredged by sail and oar.

If the area has a romantic feel, it's because the wooded banks of the Fal have been the setting for several legends, including the timeless romance of Tristan and Iseult. A kind of Cornish Lancelot and Guinevere, their tragic love story was turned into an opera by Richard Wagner, while *Castle Dor* by Sir Arthur Quiller Couch and Daphne du Maurier is also based on the legend, although moved to the 19th century and set around the River Fowey.

You will pass some steps leading foot passengers down to King Harry Ferry ❹ across the River Fal, and then cross the road that brings cars to the ferry. The chain-link ferry was initiated in 1888, replacing a manually propelled barge that previously operated on the route. Today it is owned by a syndicate of five local families. A toll is charged for the 34 cars it can carry, while a charitable donation is invited from foot passengers. Connecting Feock, Truro and Falmouth to St Mawes and the Roseland Peninsula, it avoids a 27-mile detour through Truro and Tresillian, and carries 300,000 cars every year, which is estimated to save 1.7 million kg of CO_2 and 750,000 litres of fuel.

There are several conflicting stories about how the ferry got its name. One popular legend says that King Henry VIII spent his honeymoon with Anne Boleyn at St Mawes and signed a charter for a ferry to be built on the site. However, the more likely story is that a small chapel commemorating St Mary and King Henry once stood on the Philleigh side of the passage, and the crossing took its name from this structure. The route has been voted one of the ten most scenic ferry trips in the world, along with the Staten Island Ferry in New York and the Star Ferry in Hong Kong.

The walk continues to follow the river up into North Wood on the far side of the road. We were surprised to see a large ship anchored on the bend, which looked remarkably incongruous with its surroundings. Apparently, as many as six ocean-going ships can be spotted moored here at times. This is because the Fal is actually a 'ria', a drowned river valley that was carved out by ice meltwater before the sea levels rose; much like a fjord, the water is extremely deep here. A local told us that the number of ships anchored here reflects how well the country is doing, with more ships 'moth-balled' during times of reduced global trade, like the financial crisis in the late 2000s.

The walk now takes you in along Lamouth Creek, where egrets, shelduck and kingfishers are often spotted. Before you turn, you might be able to spot Tregothnan, a country house and estate, on the hillside to the north-east. Tregothnan means the 'homestead at the head of the valley' in Cornish, and it is the location of the UK's only tea plantation. The estate has been successfully selling English tea since 2005, and 20,000 tea bushes are planted there every year.

You will come to the remains of an old jetty and a large granite post ❺, which makes a lovely swim spot. Soon after you cross the wooden bridge, another swim opportunity will come into view ❼. The steps down to it were repaired by National Trust volunteers in 2013, using granite and local hedging stone. It gives access to the foreshore, where during a lower tide you may spot wading birds like oystercatchers and curlews on the mudflats. We found an amazing variety of trees here, including beech, ash, hawthorn, hazel, chestnut, oak and cherry trees. It's a magical

place for a picnic, in the dappled light provided by the trees.

Yet another swim spot can be found down some steps at the mouth of the creek ❽ in an area that may have been used as part of the training for the Normandy landings. From 1943 until the spring of 1944, the Americans virtually took over Cornwall, with 27,000 arriving in the Fal Estuary alone. The programme of housing them all was known as Operation Bolero, and saw numerous temporary camps of bell tents. Children loved the troops, who would give them chewing gum and chocolate at the height of rationing, whilst many of the local women (and no doubt a few men as well) swooned at the arrival of so many men in uniform with exotic accents. Then it all came to an abrupt end in June of 1944, when they vanished overnight, bound for the bloody carnage of Omaha Beach, where 2,000 US soldiers lost their lives.

The walk along the north bank then passes Roundwood Fort ❾, an impressive promontory fort dating back to the Iron Age. Hidden in the woodland, this ancient scheduled monument is quite sizeable, as a walk around the perimeter will attest. We then continue down to one of the best swim spots on the walk, Roundwood Quay ❿, which dates back to the 18th century and was built to ship copper and tin ore from the Chacewater and North Downs mines. It was restored and given a new lease of life in the early 19th century, when the quayside boasted a lime house, a malthouse, a sawpit for shipbuilding and a coal yard. At one time there was even a tea garden and a boat hire business, as well as an ornamental cottage (with its own ballroom) belonging to the Daniell family, owners of Trelissick House.

With several slipways and sets of steps, it's a playful and picturesque spot to swim from. The quay sits on a point of land between Cowlands Creek on the right and Lamouth Creek on the left, with the Fal river straight ahead. We enjoyed jumping into the water (obviously checking the depth first) and then swimming around the quay to explore in both directions. The water is a lovely colour, complemented by the tree-lined banks opposite, although it was strange having views to an ocean-going vessel amongst the small sailing boats moored on the river.

Directly opposite across the River Fal you should be able to spot Tolverne Cottage, also known as Smugglers Cottage, above the boats. It was run as a tea room for many years, selling tea grown on the Tregothnan estate. It is also where General Eisenhower stayed, and a memorial stone outside commemorates the D Day landings. From the hardstanding here, 13 landing support tanks were loaded, as well as many of the 29th infantry. Meanwhile just across the Cowlands Creek around to the left is Halwyn, which boasts a small beach and the tea gardens where Churchill met Eisenhower to discuss the preparations for the invasion.

The walk back takes you up a lane and then down a bridleway, through the woods and back towards the small wooden bridge you crossed earlier ⑫. There you zig-zag up to the road, with some more marvellous views of the Fal along the way. After crossing the road, you pass the Old Lodge ⑬, which was built in 1825 to mirror the neo-classical mansion at Trelissick. It was later superseded by the imaginatively named New Lodge in 1860, when a new entrance with a grander sweep was created. Both of these are now available to rent from the National Trust, as well as four other holiday cottages around the estate.

If you have time, we would highly recommend visiting the house and gardens. Some of the plants

are extremely rare, and are a legacy of the Cornish plant hunters of the 1800s. Others that flourish in the mild climate, like the rhododendrons, were planted by the Copelands, who used the mansion as their summer house. They would pick perfect specimens of flowers and send them back to their Spode china factory in Stoke-on-Trent to be used as models for chinaware designs. You can see examples of plates in the main house.

There are some excellent facilities waiting for you at the end of the walk, including a great shop and a very affordable second-hand book shop where we uncovered all sorts of treats. There's also a fantastic gallery housed in an award-winning barn conversion, which showcases the work of local artists and craftspeople. It's run in association with the Cornwall Crafts Association. Most importantly, Crofters Café sells pasties and baked goods, as well as a lovely cup of tea.

DIRECTIONS

1 Leave the car park by the south entrance, cross into the parkland by the cattle grid and immediately take the first path downhill to the left. Where the path forks, take the right-hand fork and follow the path right past the trees down to a gate at the end, where you turn left onto the beach.
0.4 miles

2 From the beach, with your back to the sea, turn right through the black metal gate and take the path which runs around the headland by the water through the trees.
0.4 miles

3 There's a little path off where you can scramble down to the rocks for a dip, returning to keep following the path until you reach a sign that says 'Garden and House Entrance' and 'King Harry Ferry'. Follow it to the road.
0.6 miles

4 Cross the road at King Harry Ferry and take the path opposite signed 'Trelissick Woodland Walk'. Follow the path around and along the southern side of Lamouth Creek.
0.8 miles

5 Just after halfway up the creek is another swim spot, where there are the remains of an old jetty and a large granite post on the shore.
0.2 miles

6 After this you reach a junction of paths with a sign for Trelissick, Wrinkling Lane, and Roundwood Fort and Quay. Go straight on

following the pink arrow, then shortly after cross the wooden bridge on the right. You will have the water on your right.
0.8 miles

7 Soon there is another swim spot, where you see granite steps down to the shore. After your dip, carry on following the path, keeping close to the water on your right. Ignore a path to your left signed with a pink arrow. Shortly after you reach a fork, keep right here.
0.3 miles

8 You reach some steps down to another swim spot at the mouth of the creek. After a dip, return to the path.
0 miles

9 Here you hug the outer ramparts of Roundwood Fort. Continue to follow the path down to the quay, which is another fantastic swim spot.
0.1 miles

10 From Roundwood Quay, find the car parking area where you will see a gate, which looks as though it is private land and a sign on it saying it will be closed at sunset. Go through here and follow the lane past the houses, with Cowlands Creek on your right. At the end of the houses, after a short distance turn left down the bridleway and follow it all the way to the road. At the road turn left.
0.8 miles

11 After a short distance on a bend right there is a path left with

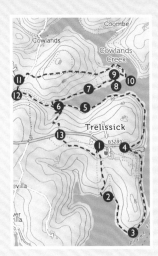

a blue sign with a horse, walker and bike on it, and a metal sign for the King Harry Ferry. Follow this track downhill, cross a stream and bear left.
0.1 miles

12 Shortly afterwards go through a wooden gate on your left with a small National Trust green metal path sign – do not follow the main track uphill. Keep following the path through the woods with the water on your left until you reach point 6 again. Here turn right to follow the zig-zag path uphill to the road and cross over through the gate.
0.6 miles

13 Pass the Old Lodge on the left, follow the path ahead until it reaches the driveway, where you turn left over the cattle grid to walk back to the start with the car park on your left.
0.4 miles

Walk 20

ST ANTHONY HEAD CIRCULAR

Take a splendidly scenic walk around the tip of the Roseland Peninsula, with both sea and river swim opportunities and the chance to visit the lighthouse from Fraggle Rock.

INFORMATION

DISTANCE: 6 miles
TIME: Allow 5 hours with swim stops
MAP: OS Explorer 105 Falmouth and Mevagissey
START POINT: National Trust Porth car park (SW 867 329, TR2 5EX).
END POINT: National Trust Porth car park.
PUBLIC TRANSPORT: Bus route 550 between Truro and St Mawes stops at Gerrans Church, near Porth. Alternatively catch a ferry from Falmouth or St Mawes to Place Quay and walk the loop from there.
SWIMMING: Towan Beach (SW 870 329), Little Molunan and Great Molunan (SW 846 316), Cellars Beach (SW 852 324), Place Quay (SW 855 322).
PLACES OF INTEREST: The battery and lighthouse on St Anthony Head, Place Manor and St Anthony church.
REFRESHMENTS: The Thirstea Company in the barn at Porth serves hot and cold, sweet and savoury treats (01872 580773, TR2 5EX).
EASIER ACCESS: Towan Beach is a short and flat walk from the car park at Porth. You could take the ferry from St Mawes to Place and swim from Place Quay or take the short walk around to Cellars Beach.
NEARBY SWIM SPOTS: Porthcurnick Beach, north of Portscatho, is a broad curve of sand with a near-legendary café above it.

Today's walk starts at Porth on the Roseland Peninsula, where there are two car parks, toilets and a café concession run by the Thirstea Company. It's then a nice easy stroll to the first swim spot at Towan Beach ❷, on Gerrans Bay. The south-east-facing beach offers something for everyone. It is sand and shingle on a high tide, while there are also rockpools to be explored if you visit on a lower tide. For the early birds, the sun rises over the sea each morning, and for those with canine swimming companions the beach is dog-friendly all year round. On an easterly wind, it can be quite exposed, with rough seas, but with the wind from the west or north, it is sheltered and a lovely spot for a dip.

As you begin your walk along the coast path you will pass a curious pole with wooden footholds that allow you to climb it. It's called the 'Wreck post' and was erected by the coastguard service to simulate a mast for use in training exercises. A rocket with a line would be fired from the 'shore' to the person up the pole on the 'sinking ship' that they would need to catch so that a lifebelt could then be hauled over to them. Having a rocket fired at you while you are up a pole isn't something we would volunteer for in a hurry.

The walk takes you up around Killigerran Head and Porthmellin Head, both offering breathtaking views. We spotted a seal pup on a beach below the cliffs, and do keep a lookout for dolphins and porpoises. Apparently both common and bottlenose dolphins have been spotted here, as well as several rarer species. Sightings of choughs are also becoming more common, which is great news as the seabirds were declared extinct in Cornwall back in the early 1970s.

During the 18th century, there was a huge decline in the population of the chough in Cornwall at the hands of 'sportsmen' and those supplying natural history specimens. However, it wasn't just trophy hunters that were responsible for the dramatic drops in numbers, but also how their clifftop habitats were managed. Sheep, cattle and ponies used to graze the cliffs, keeping the vegetation short and open and in turn providing the perfect environment for the birds to find a constant supply of soil-dwelling insects. Changes in farming practices led to the clifftop habitats becoming overgrown, which caused the chough population to leave the county.

In recent years, the clifftops have been managed more sensitively and grazing reintroduced, which led to a return of choughs to Cornwall from Wales and Ireland after a 28-year absence. A chough features on Cornwall's coat of arms, sitting proudly on top of the crest between a tin miner and a fisherman. Legend also has it that King Arthur's soul left this world in the form of a chough, its red feet and bill signifying his violent and bloody death.

The path provides stunning views down to Porthbeor Beach ❸, which means 'large cove' in Cornish. Frustratingly, a landslide a few years back has made the path down to the beach unsafe, although we did see a few people scrambling down just by the waymarker sign for St Anthony Head. The walk continues down and up a small valley before going onto St Anthony Meadow, where Shetland ponies were grazing when we visited. You'll spot a bird hide in the cliffs just before you reach Zone Point and the battery on St Anthony Head ❹.

Constructed in the late 19th century, the battery was armed until the end of the First World War and again during the Second World War. It was kept on standby until 1957, with the National Trust acquiring the site three years later. The views from here are magnificent, and a metal plaque dedicated to Maisie and Evelyn Radford gives details of what you can see. The Radford sisters started the Falmouth Opera Singers in 1923 and the Cornwall Music Festival. They set up a trust to provide grants and instrument loans to hundreds of young musicians, and the Radford Charitable Trust is still supporting musicians today.

Facing west towards Falmouth harbour, which is one of the biggest natural harbours in the world, you can spot Pendennis Castle, a mighty fortress built under Henry VIII to defend against invasion. The headland off to the left on The Lizard is Manacle Point, just behind The Manacles reef, which has been dubbed 'the grave of 1,000 ships'. On a clear day, you can see Goonhilly Earth Station in the distance. You should also be able to see the mouth of the Helford River, slightly off to the left of Falmouth. Off to the right is St Mawes Castle and then the Carrick Roads, a waterway formed from the junction of seven estuaries.

In case you were wondering, St Anthony Head has nothing to do with the man from the Nescafé adverts and *Buffy the Vampire Slayer*. It is said that Cornwall has more saints than heaven itself, with many parishes, towns, villages, churches and holy wells dedicated to these beatific men and women. Like the village of St Anthony in Roseland, the headland is named after the Italian St Antoninus, to whom the church there is dedicated – we will be visiting this pretty little church later in the walk.

We continue past the four old officers' quarters, which are now cottages available to rent from the National Trust. It's then a left turn down the hill to visit St Anthony's lighthouse **5**, built in 1835 to guide vessels clear of The Manacles rocks. From most directions the lighthouse beam is white, but in a sector close to The Manacles it is coloured red, which warns boats to steer offshore. Originally, a huge bell was also used as a fog signal, but when mains electricity was introduced in 1954 this was replaced by a modern foghorn that gives a three-second blast every 30 seconds.

If you were young in the 1980s and the lighthouse looks familiar, it's because it is Fraggle Rock lighthouse from the Jim Henson childrens' television series *Fraggle Rock*. In the show, muppet-like creatures called Fraggles, Doozers and Gorgs lived in a cave system under the lighthouse and tried to avoid the 'Silly Creatures', their name for humans. The show also had one of the best theme tunes ever and if you know it, you should definitely sing it (complete with hand claps) while you are here. Superfans can stay in Sally Port Cottage, which was the lighthouse keeper's cottage; ear plugs are provided in case the foghorn gets a bit annoying in the middle of the night, although that's part of the atmospheric adventure of staying there.

The walk then takes you down past an old paraffin store for the lighthouse, onto Little Molunan beach, which joins up with Great Molunan beach at low tide **6**. It's a great spot for a swim with views sweeping from the lighthouse across Falmouth harbour to the mouth of Carrick Roads. The beach is sandy, although completely covered by water at a high tide. It's also sheltered from easterly breezes, meaning the water is usually calm and flat here. You can scramble over the rocks and the old landing stage on the left side to discover an impressive sea cave, where we couldn't help but hope to find a Fraggle or two. It's also a perfect spot for rockpooling, while the more adventurous may like to swim in the direction of the lighthouse to explore the channels and rock formations there.

If you spot any heritage sailing boats out in the estuary, they are probably the specialised gaff cutters known as Falmouth work boats. These are oyster-dredging boats, designed to operate in shallow water and governed by ancient laws that protect the natural ecology of the river beds and the oyster stocks in the Port of Truro oyster fishery. Here engines are prohibited, and sail power and hand-pulled dredges must be used instead, the same methods of harvesting that have been employed for over 500 years. Some of these boats date back to the 1860s, and it is Europe's last commercial fleet working purely under sail.

Continuing along the coast path, towards Carricknath Point, you'll spot another charming little beach that doesn't seem to have a name, but looks reachable. The walk continues along the water's edge towards Amsterdam Point ❼, with stunning views across to the traditional fishing village of St Mawes. It then takes you downhill through a conservation area and down to Cellars Beach ❽ on the

Percuil River. The beach can be accessed through a gate and on a high tide is swimmable, although on a low tide, is just mudflats. You'll then reach the village of St Anthony in Roseland. In Cornish the village is known as Sen Anta. Roseland is thought to mean 'the land of the promontory'.

Place Manor and its church have been in the Spry family since 1649. The charming church ❾ is often open and dates back to 1150, when there was an Augustinian priory rather than a house here. Despite being extensively restored in the 19th century, it kept its original medieval cruciform plan. The church has a lovely Norman doorway, while the stained glass windows are impressive, as are the tin carvings at the top of the walls that have been painted to look like wood.

The walk continues out through the small graveyard and then down towards Place Quay ❿ from where you can swim and enjoy great views up to Place House. Some parts of the mansion date back to Tudor times, when it was built on the site of the priory, but the main house was built by the Spry family in Victorian times. They built it to resemble a French chateau, which was very fashionable at the time. Be warned, a stern sign declares the area is a private foreshore and that 'winkle picking is by permission only'.

The final leg of the walk continues along the coast past the turn-off for the Place Ferry, which crosses the river to St Mawes. The path winds up and down through some woods following the Percuil River, before turning to follow Porth Creek back to Porth, where the walk began. We think you now deserve a treat from the Thirstea Co, which is set in a converted barn at the National Trust's Porth Farm. They promise that over 97% of what they sell is "grown, made, roasted, reared, laid or churned in Cornwall". Proper job!

① Turn left out of the National Trust car park, and then follow the sign from the left of the barn for Towan Beach and your first swim spot.
0.2 miles

② From Towan Beach, turn south onto the coast path, with the sea on your left. Follow the path around Killigerran Head and Porthmellin Head.
1 mile

③ Passing a turn-off to the right with a small pointer above Porthbeor Beach, stay on the coast path through St Anthony Meadow and around Drake's Downs (ignoring any other paths). Continue on around Zone Point.
1.3 miles

④ You reach the military buildings and viewpoint at St Anthony Head. Just past the converted officers' quarters, take the footpath down to the left signposted 'Place 1¼m' and the path off left to the lighthouse on the second hairpin bend.
0.2 miles

⑤ After a look round St Anthony's lighthouse, follow the lower path on from the bend past the paraffin store on your left towards the small coves of Great Molunan and Little Molunan, which are reached by a path at the far end.
0.3 miles

⑥ From the Molunan coves, return to the coast path and turn

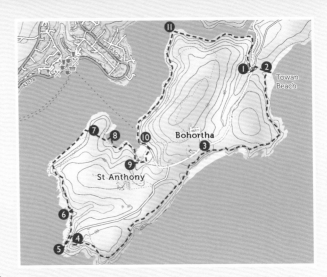

left. Continue to follow the path past Carricknath Point, and on towards Amsterdam Point.
0.8 miles

⑦ Follow the coast path away from the shore over the top of the headland at Amsterdam Point and then down onto Cellars Beach, where it is possible to swim on a high tide.
0.1 miles

⑧ From Cellars Beach, continue through the woodland and emerge at Place Manor, with the church tower visible behind it.
0.3 miles

⑨ After a look around St Anthony's church, continue through the graveyard along the footpath to the road. Turn left here and follow the road.
0.3 miles

⑩ You arrive at the stone quay opposite Place House, another potential swim spot. Rejoin the coast path on your right to follow the shoreline above the Percuil River and into the woods. Carry on along the footpath past the turn-off for the ferry, following a sign saying 'Porth Farm 1.5 miles'.
0.8 miles

⑪ Stay on the path as it rounds North Hill Point and turns east along Porth Creek, and around to the right as it reaches the causeway at Froe. Follow the sign for Porth, taking you through the trees and back to the car park.
0.7 miles

Walk 21

GORRAN HAVEN CIRCULAR

A relatively challenging but rewarding walk from harbour to high headland, taking in stunning clifftop views and swims at two wonderful isolated beaches.

INFORMATION

DISTANCE: 5 miles
TIME: Allow 4 hours
MAP: OS Explorer 105 Falmouth and Mevagissey
START POINT: Car park in Gorran Haven (SX 010 415, PL26 6JG).
END POINT: Car park in Gorran Haven.
PUBLIC TRANSPORT: Bus route 471 from St Austell ends in the village.
SWIMMING: Gorran Haven (SX 013 416), Vault Beach (SX 013 409), Hemmick Beach (SW 993 404).
PLACES OF INTEREST: Dodman Point, the Watch House, the Bulwark.
REFRESHMENTS: The Coast Path Café at Gorran Haven has great views over the sea (07512 543735, PL26 6JP). The Haven Takeaway nearby is perfect for fish and chips on the beach (01726 843555, PL26 6JG). For more substantial fare, the Barley Sheaf is just a mile up the hill (01726 843330, PL26 6HN).
EASIER ACCESS: There is direct access from the road onto the beach at Gorran Haven. Hemmick Beach can be reached via a small lane, with a National Trust car park at Penare.
NEARBY SWIM SPOTS: Colona Beach is a pretty and little-known sandy beach about an hour's walk east from Gorran Haven towards Mevagissey. Porthluney Cove and Caerhays Castle are also worth a visit.

Our walk begins and ends in the attractive coastal village of Gorran Haven ❶, where a cluster of whitewashed fishermen's cottages guard the secluded cove. Here you will find two sandy beaches, Gorran Beach and Little Perhaver, separated by rocks that you can walk around on a lower tide or swim around on a high tide. The charming village is understandably popular in the summer months, sitting as it does in the lee of the 114-metre Dodman Point to the west. This means the beaches are relatively sheltered, making them ideal for families. Dogs are also welcome, although they must be kept on leads between Easter and September.

Gorran Haven was a medieval fishing harbour known as Portheast, or in Cornish Porthust, a corruption of Porth Just, meaning Just's Cove. Indeed, one of the two churches in the village is dedicated to St Just, although the building was also used as a fish cellar for over a century. This was an important port for 'seining' pilchards using long nets, which was first recorded here in the 13th century.

The first pier was built in the 15th century, and during the 18th and 19th centuries the port was a landing place for merchandise brought in from Fowey by barge. By the end of the 19th century fishing had declined, although the building of the quay you see today in 1888 did lead to it becoming an important place for landing crab and lobster. Sadly, the industry never really recovered following the Second World War; there are still a handful of working boats, but many of them are now used for tourist fishing trips over the summer months.

The route takes you up out of the village and onto a spectacular stretch of coast path with lofty views back down to Gorran Haven. As the path hugs the shoulder of the National Trust land at Lamledra, you should be able to see the Gwineas rocks out at sea. They take their name from the Cornish words 'gwyn' and 'enys' meaning holy or white island. The undulating path climbs and falls through craggy coastal grasslands, where wild flowers perfectly complement the emerald waters during the spring and summer months. On a clear day you can see back to the tower on Gribben Head near Fowey and as far as Rame Head near Plymouth.

Just after you walk down some steps and start heading up the path towards a natural lookout point, a fisherman's path goes off to the left. It's quite steep, but you will be rewarded with a natural playground for jumping and exploring down at what is known as Pen-a-maen or Maenease Point ❸. Local legend has it that at sunrise, the silhouette of a mermaid brushing her hair can sometimes be seen on the shelf of rocks found here. It's a wonderful place to play at highish water, with platforms to jump from, rocks to conquer and gulleys to explore.

Soon you will be able to see Little Sand Cove below, which can be reached by swimming from our first dipping spot at Vault Beach ❺, around the next headland. It's a picturesque walk down to the mile-long strand, which is also known as Bow Beach because of its curve. From a distance it looks like a sandy beach, but when you reach it you find it is actually fine shingle that has been ground down from the Devonian slate over 400 million years. Being somewhat isolated, the beach is often deserted; the far end of the cove, past the white cross painted on the cliff, is actually a designated nudist area.

On a low tide it's fun to enter the clear turquoise waters and swim off to the left to explore amongst the channels between the rocks. Incidentally, the beach features in Richard Curtis' time travel romance *About Time*. It's supposed to be at the bottom of the garden of the family home, although the house filmed is actually Porthpean House, some 8 miles up the coast.

Above the far end of the beach you will be able to see the striking Dodman Point ❽, which is the highest point in South Cornwall. Just looking at it from sea level, you know it is going to be a strenuous but rewarding climb. You'll get more of the stunning views you have come to expect on this walk before eventually reaching the Point itself, where there is a large cross ❽. This was built back in 1896 by the Reverend George Martin of Caerhays as a navigation aid for shipping – it is telling that the earlier name for the point was the Deadman. Apparently, this is also one of the points around the English coast where Jehovah's Witnesses intend to congregate on the day of Armageddon, so if there is a large crowd there when you arrive, it might be time to panic.

The views are simply extraordinary, and on a clear day you can see right along the south coast from Bolt Head in Devon to the east and over to the Lizard in the west. Turning around you can also spot Bodmin Moor and Dartmoor in the distance. The Bulwark ❾ is a long ditch that spans the headland, defining it as an unusually large Iron Age promontory fort. The small hut near the cross is called The Watch House and was established as a signal station in 1795 as part of the Napoleonic War defences. It was built on the former site of a Spanish Armada beacon site, and has also been used to watch for smugglers bringing their contraband to shore.

The National Trust grazes Dexter cattle and Dartmoor ponies here to help control the coarse scrub and to allow more delicate species to flourish. As a result, expect to see blankets of wildflowers if you visit during the spring and summer. This is a great place to spot both kestrels and peregrines circling above, looking for prey. It's a lovely but steep walk as you make your way down the other hillside, before Hemmick Beach ❿ eventually comes into view. With no car park at the beach, you should be in for another fairly quiet swim stop.

In his chapter of *My Cornwall*, an anthology about the county published in 1971, writer Colin Wilson said that walking enthusiasts "will discover one of the pleasantest beaches in the area, Hemmick. Because of its enormous rocks – with narrow passageways between some of them – Hemmick has a fairy-tale quality, and children love it… By the time you have walked from one end to the other (preferably at low tide – there are parts where you can easily be caught by a rising tide), and the children have scrambled over rocks and explored small 'caves' and paddled in the tide pools, everyone is ready for tea, and you have that virtuous feeling that comes from taking exercise."

Add a swim and you can feel even more virtuous. Off to the left on a higher tide there are some great rock formations and channels to explore before enjoying a picnic on the beach. On a lower tide you can walk past the rocky outcrops to Helencane Cove to the left and Percunning Cove to the right. The charming cottage overlooking the beach belongs to the National Trust and can be rented; the two-bedroom property would make an ideal spot for a remote wild swimming break, although you can only feel it

might have been a bit cramped when back in 1881 it housed the local blacksmith, Simon Liddicoat and his wife Mary – along with their six children!

After turning slightly back on yourself, the path takes you up another hill and past Penare Farm ⓫, where they rear Dexter cattle, and the National Trust car park for the Dodman. The Trust has several holiday rentals here including Granny's Cottage, which takes its name from Granny Whetter, the matriarch of the local farming family, and a converted barn called Edgcumbe. After walking along the lanes for a short while, a path takes you across some fields and through the middle of Treveague Farm Campsite ⓭. As well as camping and touring sites, the farm also rents out cottages. Keep an eye out for the china clay pits in the distance, the spoil heaps of which have been dubbed the Cornish Alps.

The walk takes you around the rear of some houses (see if you can resist a go on the swings made from old buoys hanging from the trees) and then eventually back down into Gorran Haven, turning right to take you back to the car park. If you are feeling in need of serious refreshment, why not head up to The Barley Sheaf in nearby Gorran Churchtown. Back in 1837, local farmer William Kendall was so badly behaved that he managed to get himself banned from all of the pubs in the area. To solve this problem (and to quench his daily thirst), he decided to open his own pub, which has stayed in the family ever since and is now run by his great-great-great grandson.

DIRECTIONS

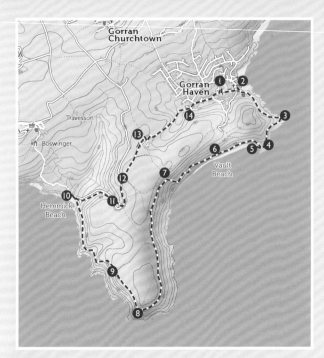

❶ From the car park, turn left and walk down the road to the beach.
0.1 miles

❷ At the Haven fish and chip shop, turn right into Foxhole Lane and then head up the stone steps to follow the coast path with the sea on your left. After a while the path bends around to the left and dips down some steps, then climbs for a short distance to a small headland, which looks like a lookout point.
0.4 miles

❸ Just before the brow of Pen-a-maen/Maenease Point, there is a path to the left where

you can scramble down and swim off the rocks below. Return to the coast path and continue.
0.2 miles

❹ As the path rounds the next headland and you look towards Vault Beach, there is a fork. Take the left fork down to the beach.
0.1 miles

❺ From Vault Beach, start back on the path up and you will see some steps shortly on the left. Ascend here to re-join the coast path and walk along with the beach below on your left, keeping left at any forks.
0.3 miles

❻ The path continues along the clifftop and forks about half-way along; take the left fork and go through a gateway to continue along the coast path.
0.4 miles

❼ You reach a kissing gate with a finger-post for the coast path and Dodman Point. Go through and follow the path around the headland. Keep following signs for Dodman Point and walk around the outside of the headland to the western side.
0.9 miles

❽ A right turn off the path takes you on a short detour to visit the Watch Hut. From here, continue along the coast path and stop to admire the huge cross.
0.4 miles

❾ You come to an unusual stile that looks like something out of the Wild West; this is the western end of the Bulwark, and if you want to explore the Iron Age remains this is a good place to detour, returning to this point. Otherwise, keep on the main path following the sign for the coast path and Hemmick to emerge down steps onto the road by the beach. Head left to the beach.
0.7 miles

❿ From Hemmick Beach, go back the way you came, up the steps and through the gate back into the field, but turn left following the sign for Penare car park. Walk parallel to the road to the top of the field, and go through the

wooden gate with the National Trust sign on it.
0.4 miles

⓫ At Penare, bear left following the sign for the car park down to the road; do not go straight on following the sign for Dodman Point. Walk along the road with the car park on your left, and follow the road around to the left, ignoring a footpath sign for Gorran Haven to the right.
0.2 miles

⓬ You will reach a junction on a bend left, with a wooden five-bar gate and a public footpath sign in front of you. Go straight ahead, leaving the road, and follow through a metal gate and the campsite.
0.3 miles

⓭ Turn right out of Treveague Farm Campsite, following the sign for Gorran Haven past Treveague Farm on your right. Turn left at the sign for Gorran Haven to walk between two houses (don't worry if it feels as though you're trespassing; you're not), and follow the path past the unusual buoy swings and downhill towards Gorran Haven.
0.4 miles

⓮ The path emerges among houses, where you bear right along the driveway, then left following the footpath sign with a yellow arrow, to the road. Turn right into the road and follow it back to the car park.
0.3 miles

Walk 22

CHARLESTOWN CIRCULAR

An adventurous walk starting and finishing at the historic port of Charlestown, with spectacular clifftop views. You can swim at two beaches, or even from beach to beach with a drybag-towfloat or someone to carry your stuff on shore.

Charlestown ❶ is a charming UNESCO World Heritage Site with a fascinating history. It was built between 1790 and 1810 as a Georgian 'new town' by Charles Rashleigh, who gave his name to the port, and designed by John Smeaton, who also built the Eddystone Rock lighthouse (now on Plymouth Hoe). Created to export copper from nearby mines and later china clay, it remained busy for almost two centuries. Various other industries sprang up around the harbour, including boat-builders, brickworks, lime kilns, rope makers and fish curers.

Although the last shipment of clay left the port in 2000, the town has gained a new lease of life as both a film location and tourist attraction. Television and movie productions filmed in the privately owned harbour include *The Eagle Has Landed*, *The Three Musketeers*, *Alice in Wonderland*, *Doctor Who* and *Saving Private Ryan*. Most recently, the BBC series *Poldark* has used Charlestown as a location, and the multi-award-winning film *Bait* was filmed here. Shot on a vintage 16mm camera in black and white, it portrays the tensions between locals and wealthy incomers.

It's worth allowing a bit of time either before or after your swim walk to explore the Grade-II-listed harbour and perhaps even take a tour of the town's resident tall ship, the *Kasjamoor*. The Shipwreck and Heritage Centre is also well worth a visit, housing some 8,000 artefacts from over 150 shipwrecks. There's also a great selection of places to eat and drink – and of course buy Poldark souvenirs.

From a picturesque start at the harbour, the route continues on a long lane past a few housing estates and then a rather unremarkable road. But don't worry, the walk more than makes up for it with

INFORMATION

DISTANCE: 3 miles
TIME: Allow at least 5 hours to enjoy swims at both Porthpean and Duporth and perhaps a third at Charlestown, which is great to explore.
MAP: OS Explorer 105 Falmouth and Mevagissey
START POINT: Charlestown car park (SX 038 517, PL25 3NH).
END POINT: Charlestown car park
PUBLIC TRANSPORT: Bus routes 21 between Newquay and St Austell and 24 between Fowey and St Austell both stop in Charlestown.
SWIMMING: Porthpean Beach (SX 032 507), Duporth Beach (SX 035 512), Charlestown (SX 039 514), optional extra Black Head (SX 038 481).
PLACES OF INTEREST: Charlestown harbour and Shipwreck and Heritage Centre, Higher Porthpean, Carrickowel Point.
REFRESHMENTS: Seasonal beach café at Porthpean (01726 69080, PL26 6AU). Eateries in Charlestown: the Boathouse (01726 63322, PL25 3NJ) and the Pier House, which is dog friendly and has lovely views over the harbour (01726 67955, PL25 3NJ).
EASIER ACCESS: Charlestown harbour and beach are very near the car park. There is also a car park very close to the beach at Porthpean.
NEARBY SWIM SPOTS: Hallane Beach (not named on OS map, but below Hallane Mill) beyond Black Head south of Porthpean is remote and has a waterfall. Further south, Polstreath Beach has clear water (30-minute walk from Mevagissey harbour).

stunning views a bit further along. Once you join the bridleway that borders the golf club and takes you through a tunnel of trees, things start to get interesting. At the end of the track, the walk heads down into the coastal hamlet of Higher Porthpean, with Porthpean being Cornish for 'little cove'.

There's a charming small church ❹ dedicated to St Levan, the Cornish patron saint of fishermen. The village once formed part of the Penrice Estate and was owned by the Sawle family, who built the church as a private family chapel. When the last of the family line died in 1971, it was given to St Austell parish. When we visited we were fortunate enough to meet the vicar and some of the congregation, who kindly offered us a cream tea and told us about plans they had to be serving tea and cakes from the small garden at the front of the church in the near future.

While you can walk straight down to the beach through Lower Porthpean from here, we take a small diversion through what looks like someone's private drive and through some giant rhubarb plants, up onto the hillside for glorious views down towards our two swimming beaches. Also look out for the offshore mussel farm, where blue mussels are grown on ropes suspended between buoys. After joining the coast path, the route then drops down past Porthpean Sailing Club and down onto the beach ❼.

This is a lovely shallow beach to swim from. Unfortunately, it is only dog friendly from the end of September to Easter, although they are fine on the upper path by the café. It is best to swim from the left-hand side of the beach if you fancy a bit of exploration, because there are some great rocks and islets at this end to swim around and climb on.

Look out for the Coffin Cave in the cliff on the left-hand side. Some say it was cut by smugglers

in the 18th century, others that it was a failed exploratory mine level; either way, you can still see pick marks. It has two chambers handy for hiding contraband and once had a larger rock in front of it that hid the entrance. At high tide it could only be accessed by rowing boat, although we did manage to scramble in to check if they had left any rum. Sadly, they hadn't.

If you are confident swimmer, it is fun to swim on from here to Duporth Beach ❽ and Charlestown. If you're with friends they can carry your stuff and meet you at the next waterside location, or you can use a drybag-towfloat. It's about 0.3 miles from Porthpean to Duporth, and the same again from Duporth to Charlestown; you could swim either leg or both.

The walk continues up the steps at the far side of the beach and past a lookout tower at Carrickowel Point, which was used by RAF Coastal Command for practice bombing during the Second World War. There were two large wooden targets floating 2 miles out in St Austell Bay and also a moving

target towed by what we can only think were a very brave crew from Fowey.

Following some more great views, the route then takes you down to Duporth Beach. Part of the village here was a holiday village resort for most of the 20th century, and before that the estate of the same Charles Rashleigh who built Charlestown. The new Two Coves residential development on the site of the resort features houses built in a traditional Cornish style that have a gated access to the beach, which is privately owned but with public access from the coast path. At high tide there is actually very little beach, but at mid to low tide there is lots of sand, and rock pools.

You can scramble over the rocks at a low tide to Charlestown, but of course it is more fun to swim around past a secret beach and get a unique view of the harbour. There are islets of rock to

swim between or conquer as you head towards the headland, and quite a sizeable cave to explore when you land at Charlestown. If this area takes your fancy, you could return for the annual 5k swim from Charlestown to Polkerris, organised by Mad Hatter Sports Events.

If you're walking, you need to continue along the coast path back to Charlestown, either past or through the cliff battery. This was constructed on behalf of Charles Rashleigh around 1793 to defend his new harbour, and his estate workers formed a company of artillery volunteers who held regular gun drills here. The views down to Charlestown are impressive from here and we would highly recommend trying to spot which local establishment you will be buying your well-deserved Cornish pasty from once you have dropped back down into the village.

CHARLESTOWN EXTENSION

From Porthpean **6** you can walk on south along the coast path to Black Head. It's about 1.9 miles each way, along cliff tops and through woods and fields before emerging into the old hillfort that marks the top of Black Head. From here you get a fantastic view east and west along miles of coast, and you can also drop down a path to a beach on the west side of Black Head. If you prefer just this Black Head loop, Porthpean has a car park just above the beach, or there's a car park near the end of the single-track dead-end road to Trenarren/Black Head, about 0.7 miles on the coast path from the head itself.

DIRECTIONS

1 Turn right out of the car park and walk towards the harbour, before turning a hairpin right into Barkhouse Lane. Walk to the end and go through the staggered fence opening, bearing left onto the pavement with railings on Duporth Road. Stay on this pavement to the end, crossing over and ignoring any turns into housing estates and passing a post box and traffic calming point.
0.7 miles

2 At the staggered crossroads at the end of the road, turn left onto Porthpean Road, following the sign for Little Harbour. Follow the pavement past the community hospital on the right, crossing over the turning for Ridgewood Close, and then turn left onto Porthpean Beach Road. About 130 metres along, there is a bridleway on your right opposite a house called Caislin – be careful as it is easy to miss.
0.3 miles

3 Turn right into the bridleway and stay on it past the golf course. At the end you reach a lane where you turn left. Continue down Porthpean Beach Road until you reach the church on your left.
0.4 miles

4 With St Levan's church entrance directly behind you, walk onto the track beside Ivy Cottage and follow this down to the driveway of Trelowen. Go through the gate into the turning area and head for the garage on your right. There is a kissing gate to the left of the garage.
0.1 miles

5 Go through the kissing gate and then follow the right-hand side of the field up the hill, where you will find a gap leading into the next field. Go through the gap into the left field and follow the hedge on your right to reach a granite post and a waymark.
0.2 miles

6 From the granite post, turn left downhill to a kissing gate. Go through this and then turn left onto the coast path. After a stile, you will go down some steps and then reach Porthpean Sailing Club. Follow the path down to the beach.
0.3 miles

7 From Porthpean Beach, climb the steps at the far end of the sea wall. Continue along the path and up a flight of steps until you reach a lookout tower. Follow the coast path with the sea on your right until you reach Duporth Beach.
0.4 miles

8 From Duporth Beach, retrace your steps to the coast path and turn right to cross the small bridge. Pass an iron kissing gate and continue down past Crinnis Cliff Battery. Either walk through the battery (it re-joins the path) or continue along the path. Walk down a flight of steps, through a kissing gate and on until you reach Charlestown Harbour. Another swim is possible here, before heading back up through the village to the car park where you started.
0.5 miles

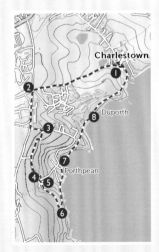

165

READYMONEY BEACH TO POLRIDMOUTH FIGURE OF EIGHT

A stunning coastal walk through Daphne du Maurier country, with two picturesque swims from glorious sandy beaches en route and the chance for some liquid refreshment towards the end in the charming town of Fowey.

INFORMATION

DISTANCE: 5.6 miles
TIME: Allow at least 6 hours
MAP: OS Explorer 107 St Austell and Liskeard
START POINT: Car park in Readymoney (SX 116 513, PL23 1DG).
END POINT: Car park in Readymoney
PUBLIC TRANSPORT: Bus routes 24 and 25 run from Par station to Fowey.
SWIMMING: Polridmouth (SX 102 503), Readymoney Beach (SX 118 511).
PLACES OF INTEREST: Readymoney Beach, St Catherine's Castle, Polridmouth Cottage, The Gribbin Headland Daymark, Fowey town, St Fimbarrus Church, Fowey Hall.
REFRESHMENTS: The seasonal Beach Shop at Readymoney Cove sells coffee hand-roasted in Cornwall, pasties and ice-cream (07980 311646, PL23 1JH). Fowey Harbour Hotel serves a cream tea with views (01726 832551, PL23 1HX). On the quay, find The Haveners (01726 834591, PL23 1AT) and the King of Prussia (01726 833694, PL23 1AT).
EASIER ACCESS: A 0.3-mile walk from the car park to Readymoney Cove, with disabled toilets during the season. Polridmouth Cove (follow signs for Menabilly on the A3082 to Fowey (PL24 2TN) has a car park at the road end, an 0.6-mile walk down an unmade track.
NEARBY SWIM SPOTS: Lansallos Cove is a pretty, secluded beach (National Trust car park nearby). Polkerris, west of Fowey, has a sandy beach down a lane past Kilmarth, home of Daphne du Maurier. Just off the eastern end of the wide Par Sands is Kilmarth/Booley Beach, for a quieter dip.

T his walk begins at Readymoney Cove ❷, a sheltered beach with impressive views over the mouth of the River Fowey estuary. Its name may sound enigmatic, lucrative and straight out of a pirate adventure, but its origins have nothing to do with buried treasure. It's believed that the cove was once called Redeman, from the Cornish for 'pebbly ford', and the name has altered over the years – in Cornish it is now Porth Mundy. You would however need seriously ready money to afford any of the properties that overlook the beach, including the imposing Point Neptune House, built in the mid-19th century by William Rashleigh. The lane from the car park to this point is part of St Catherine's Parade, which was built by William Rashleigh for access to the mansion, and named after his wife.

The Rashleigh family owned nearby Menabilly, the one time home of Daphne du Maurier, one of several connections to the author that will be revealed along today's walk. When William inherited the estate in 1855, he decided that as a seafaring man he would prefer to live by the shore and so built Point Neptune. Indeed, the gates to the house once stood at the entrance to Menabilly. The cottage directly behind the beach was once the stables and carriage house for Point Neptune, and was where du Maurier lived in 1942 and wrote *Hungry Hill*, before moving to Menabilly itself in 1943.

While it might be tempting to go straight for a dip, the walk returns here later, so instead we will be heading to the right up to St Catherine's Castle ❸, which overlooks the beach. The castle, named after the headland upon which it stands, was built in response to the threat of invasion by France and the Holy Roman Empire following Henry VIII's divorce from Catherine of Aragon. The fort was modified in the 19th century during the Crimean War, while during the Second World War it was used to house an anti-aircraft gun and ammunition. Today it is managed by English Heritage and is free to enter.

The views up the estuary to Fowey Harbour are impressive. Across the mouth of the river you can see the town of Polruan, and you might be able to spot the stack-shaped ruins of St Saviour's Chapel, dating to the 8th or 9th century. It was a prominent landmark for sailors, and at night a beacon would be lit in the tower to guide mariners. It fell into disrepair following the dissolution of the monasteries.

On the cliffs below, look out for Punches Cross, another navigational aid which was probably built to mark the limit of the jurisdiction of the monks from the priory of Tywardreath. One improbable legend says that Joseph of Arimathea brought his nephew – a young Jesus – to Britain and they landed on the rocks here, climbing up the hill to where the chapel of St Saviour's was built.

Look out also for the block house, one of a pair on either side of the river, built when the Hundred Years War turned against the English, and guns and cannons failed to stop a French raid on Fowey in 1457. A thick chain was stretched between the two towers, which could be dropped to the seabed when friendly vessels sailed past, but raised during enemy attack. The chain was confiscated by Edward VI and given to Dartmouth Castle (which had similar defences in place) following a falling out with two Fowey locals. Ironically, Comedienne Dawn French lives in Fowey, with 'dawn' and 'French' definitely not a pair of words you would have wanted to have heard together in the 15th century.

The walk continues along the coast path across Allday's Fields, which used to be The Fowey Golf Club until the land was requisitioned during the Second World War. See if you can also spot the red of St Catherine's Lighthouse through the trees on the cliff edge. The walk passes Penventinue Cove and later drops down to Coombe Hawne ❹, which could make an extra swim spot. You won't be surprised to hear that both of these wild and atmospheric coves have attracted pirates and smugglers. Soon the striped tower at Gribbin Head will come into view in the distance, the ultimate goal and halfway point of the walk. If a flag is flying from the top, it means the tower is open and you can climb it.

The walk then drops down to Polridmouth ❺, which the locals pronounce 'Pridmuth'. It's a truly charming spot with a delightful cottage, manicured lawns and an ornamental lake that is separated from the beach by a dam, with stepping stones you can cross. Built in the 1920s, incredibly the lake was used in the Second World War as a decoy Fowey Harbour to confuse enemy aircraft. Borrowing film set techniques developed at Shepperton Studios, more than 1,100 imitation airfields, towns and ports were created across the country, each a few miles from the real thing.

Fowey was considered a target as more than 2,000 US Navy personnel were stationed in the town in preparation for D-day. At least one bomb is known to have been drawn away from the main town by the decoy site, while it is estimated that around 5% of German bombs were diverted by dummy stage sets across the UK, saving thousands of lives.

The beach here is also sometimes known as Menabilly, because the Georgian mansion of that name is hidden up the wooded valley behind the lakes. Apparently, in the 1920s, Daphne du Maurier followed the same route as we are and trespassed to look at the then dilapidated and usually empty house. It was an inspiration for Manderley in her most famous book, *Rebecca*. She wrote the book while stationed with her husband in Alexandria, Egypt, and the famous opening line, "Last night, I dreamt I went to Manderley again" can be read as her homesickness for Cornwall. The book was so successful that she was able to lease the house from the Rashleigh family in 1943. She lived there for over 20 years, also featuring the house in *The King's General*.

The little cottage by the beach was built on the site of an old water mill that supplied the Menabilly estate with grain. Today it is a holiday let, but it is believed to have been the inspiration for the boathouse in *Rebecca*. Daphne loved the sea and would walk the mile down the drive with her children to swim every day and sometimes twice in the summer. It's a lovely area to swim from and at high tide we would suggest walking around the small headland and past the honesty fridge (with ice-creams and cold drinks) to swim from the sandy beach there ❻.

The water is crystal clear, while on a low tide the cove is split in two by a rocky outcrop that makes for some perfect rock pooling adventures. Also on a low tide you may spot the rusting remains of the *Romanie*, a three-masted cargo ship that ran aground in January 1930, with no loss of life. The wreck inspired du Maurier to make the beach the setting for Rebecca's mysterious death. Save some energy following your swim for the strenuous climb up to the tower.

The Gribbin Headland Daymark was constructed in 1832 as a navigational aid for sailors, to mark the entrance to Fowey Harbour and ensure they didn't mistake the treacherous shallows of St Austell Bay for the deep waters of Falmouth harbour. William Rashleigh of nearby Menabilly donated the land, asking that the beacon should also be an ornament to his grounds – hence the striking Greco-Gothic square tower, now in the hands of the National Trust. The tower is open every Sunday from July to early August, and 109 steps lead to some stunning views, although the panorama from the base of the tower is almost equally impressive. While you retrace your steps back down the hill, see if you can glimpse Menabilly through the trees up behind Polridmouth. The famous house is completely private, and the only other opportunity to see the inspiration for Manderley is to book one of the holiday cottages in the grounds. The walk returns in front of the ornamental lake and then up the hill, crossing to the rear of Allday's Fields, before dropping quite steeply to join The Saints Way back down to Readymoney Cove. By now, you should be ready for a dip, with a floating platform to swim out to during the summer months.

When you are suitably refreshed, have a look for the old lime kiln. It was built to produce lime for building at Menabilly, with the turrets (resembling upside-down ice-cream cones) probably added on top when Point Neptune was built. When Point Neptune was sold in 1935, the kiln was converted into a storeroom. A public shelter and toilets were also added, which now form the café. It's well worth stopping for a drink here or perhaps a delicious Cornish ice-cream.

The walk continues past the rear of Point Neptune and along the seafront. It's a truly stunning walk with some incredible viewing points along the way, taking you via the esplanade right into the medieval heart of Fowey itself. Consider popping into Bookends of Fowey to grab a copy of a Daphne du Maurier classic to enjoy, and then you have definitely earned some refreshments – perhaps at The Haveners or The King of Prussia, with river views.

The walk continues up through the churchyard of St Fimbarrus Church ❿, which marks the end of the Saints Way you were walking along earlier. This drover's route was originally followed by both pilgrims and merchants and stretches all the way to Padstow. St Finbarr, the first bishop of Cork, took the route on his way to Rome and stopped to build a small church. It was replaced by a Norman church and then the present church, although the font still remains from the Norman period. If the church is open, look out for the 500-year-old

wagon roof and the 400-year-old pulpit made from the panelling of a Spanish Galleon.

As you head back to Readymoney Cove car park you will pass the secluded Fowey Hall, built in 1892 as a country retreat for Charles Hanson, who later became Lord Mayor of London and a baronet. A regular guest at the mansion was Kenneth Grahame, and it is widely believed that it inspired Toad Hall in *The Wind in the Willows*, with Fowey itself depicted by the Sea Rat as 'the little grey sea town... that clings along one steep side of the harbour. There through dark doorways you look down flights of stone steps, overhung by great pink tufts of valerian and ending in a patch of sparkling blue water'. The eight bedrooms in the courtyard are named in memory of the animals in his beloved tale. Today it is a hotel and also hosted the wedding of local resident Dawn French to Mark Bignell. It's now back to the start before you return home. But we are sure it won't be long until you dream of Fowey again…

GRIBBEN HEAD EXTENSION (ABOUT 3.7 MILES)

From Gribben Head, you can walk north along the coast path almost to Polkerris with the expanse of St Austell Bay to your left, and views across to Black Head. About 1.5 miles past the tower at Gribben Head, and just over a stile, you'll find a little path down to a tiny beach (SX 092 517) for a swim. Another 500 metres on you have a choice of dropping down through the woods to visit Polkerris village, or turning inland and, after a walk across a field, joining the well-signed Saints Way through lanes and fields back to Fowey.

1 Exit the car park from the bottom left corner (looking from the entrance), turning left onto a lane that takes you down to Neptune House, then turning right onto the road to the beach.
0.3 miles

2 Walk around the rear of Readymoney Cove and follow the sign for the coast path past the cottages and up into the valley, turning left at the waymark by the wooden fence. When the path splits, bear left following the slate sign for Gribben.
0.2 miles

3 At the St Catherine's Castle sign, bear left if you want to visit the castle or continue right. Then take the middle path past the shelter up to your right and follow it to another junction with a gate to the left. Go through the gate and continue along the coast path across Allday's Fields and then through a stile. Follow the steps down to the back of the cove.
0.4 miles

4 Continue from Coombe Hawne cove past the waymark, over a stone stile and through a gate, following the path along the edge of the fields. Go through several gates and fields before the striped tower at Gribbin Head comes into view. Follow the steps down towards Polridmouth.
0.8 miles

5 Pass the sign for Coombe Farm to cross the stepping stones near Polridmouth Cottage and ornamental lake. Follow the path around to the next beach for a swim.
0.1 miles

6 From the beach, follow the path up the hill to the tower at Gribbin Head.
0.5 miles

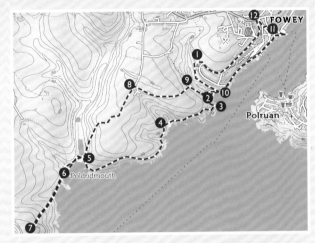

7 Once you have enjoyed the views from the Gribben Head Daymark, walk back down the path to Polridmouth and return to point 5, the waymark for Coombe Farm. Turn left to follow the path through one gate, then another, and follow the right hedge past one field gate to reach a pedestrian gate.
1.2 miles

8 You reach a junction of tracks and lanes. Take the one signposted for Readymoney (second right). Follow it across the parking area onto the gravel path and then through a gate. Continue diagonally across the field taking the right-hand gate in the far corner, and then turn left to follow the hedge to a metal kissing gate. Follow the path downhill through the trees, keeping right at any forks, to reach a waymark.
0.4 miles

9 Turn right and follow the path to another waymark that you will recognise from earlier. Turn left to follow the path back down to Readymoney Cove (point 2).
0.2 miles

10 From the beach, walk around the rear of Neptune House and onto Readymoney Road. This eventually becomes the Esplanade which will take you right into the town centre. Turn right at the Ship Inn past the Aquarium to the Town Quay. Enjoy a drink before walking back towards the pub.
0.7 miles

11 Head into the churchyard and visit the church. Continue through the churchyard and turn left onto Cobbs Well and right onto Lostwithiel street. Walk up by the Safe Harbour Inn.
0.2 miles

12 Turn left down Hanson Drive at the T junction, and turn left to stay on it after about 150 metres, following the sign for Readymoney. Look out for the gates of Fowey Hall on your right and glimpses through the trees. Hanson Drive curves right then eventually bends left and becomes Tower Park, and then you are back at the car park.
0.6 miles

Walk 24

LANHYDROCK AND RESPRYN BRIDGE CIRCULAR

The heart of Cornwall offers woodland walks, a stately home and ample swimming opportunities in the sparkling waters of the River Fowey.

INFORMATION

DISTANCE: 5 miles
TIME: 5 hours for swims and a picnic
MAP: OS Explorer 107 St Austell & Liskeard
START POINT: National Trust car park at Lanhydrock (SX 087 643, PL30 4AB), free for members, but advance booking may be necessary.
END POINT: National Trust car park at Lanhydrock.
PUBLIC TRANSPORT: Bodmin Parkway station is 1.75 miles by cycle or on foot, and the route passes fairly close to it, if you want to start there.
SWIMMING: Bodmin Road Viaduct (SX 108 641), piskie dust bridge (SX 106 641), river bend (SX 104 639), Respryn Bridge (SX 099 635), Higginsmoor Wood (SX 096 627).
PLACES OF INTEREST: Respryn Bridge, Lanhydrock House, Victorian swimming pool.
REFRESHMENTS: The Park Café (National Trust) near the car park at Lanhydrock House offers food and refreshments (01208 265950, PL30 5AD). The 18th-century Lanivet Inn is one of the oldest run by the St Austell Brewery (01208 831 212 PL30 5ET).
EASIER ACCESS: Small National Trust car park at Respryn Bridge. The bank leads down to a fairly accessible shingle area; wade through the shallow water to reach the deeps.
NEARBY SWIM SPOTS: Lerryn on the Fowey estuary is lovely to swim at high tide. The quay at the church of St Winnow is great for a high tide dip. Talland Bay has twin beaches and is good for swimming at all tides.

Today's jaunt is a truly adventurous walk through some of the 900 acres of land surrounding Lanhydrock House, a beautiful family home on the upper banks of the River Fowey that has been owned by the National Trust since 1953. The Trust are very keen that people get out and enjoy the grounds and have created a number of walking trails, as well as 6 miles of cycling routes (you can also hire bikes), while you can swim in the river at various picturesque spots. The walk starts by the main car park, where there are also toilets and a café, as well as a visitor centre. It's then off into the woods and past the Cycling Skills Area, for those looking to improve their two-wheeled technique.

You'll head down through Costislost Plantation, which was once part of Costislost, a 17th-century farm just the other side of Bodmin that today is run as a luxury bed and breakfast. The walk continues down through Hart Wood, where you'll pass beneath many beeches, among other broadleaf trees. Keep an eye out for the historic deer wall that used to surround the old estate, built to discourage the deer from leaving the park. Red, roe and fallow deer still venture into the woods here and can sometimes be spotted in the early morning, before the dog walkers arrive.

The walk reaches the river, crossing a bridge and continuing down through Dreasonmoor Wood to the first swim. It's a really picturesque spot under the Bodmin Road Viaduct ❻, which carries the Bodmin & Wenford line from Bodmin Parkway station along a 13-mile route up to Boscarne Junction, on the edge of Bodmin Moor. The line was opened in 1834 to transport minerals and agricultural sea sand, and runs today as a heritage railway.

There are tiny glittering specks on the river bed along this stretch that are almost certainly the product of tin-rich soil in the area. We nicknamed it Cornish piskie dust, although we have no evidence that is what it actually is. Almost as elusive as piskies are kingfishers and otters, who can apparently be spotted playing in these waters. Dippers and wagtails are also common, and at dusk you may be fortunate enough to spot Daubenton's bats. A second potential dipping spot is a short walk away, under another attractive single-arch bridge ❺. The dappled light on the Cornish ale-coloured water is magical, as are the specks glinting below.

The walk then continues down the scenic river bank. Look out for salmon and sea trout darting past in the waters. Signs advise that dogs should only enter the waters at designated points due to the erosion of the banks. The same can be said for humans – you should really only swim from areas with natural beaches around here, rather than scrambling down the banks. It's fun testing your knowledge of trees along this walk; along the river and up into the Great Wood you will be able to count beech, sycamore, oak, ash, sweet chestnut, holly and Scots pine. We also spotted some amazing fungi growing on the trees.

The next swim was our favourite, found on the bend in the river ❽ and resembling something from a Mark Twain novel. A rope swing dangled temptingly from the branches of a lovely old tree whose branches spread out over the river, while there was the possibility to swoosh at the far side, where the waters were running faster. The mainline railway track passes by here, and you may reflect that gently floating on your back, drifting along with the river, is far preferable to an overcrowded train. You may want to keep your swimming costume on from here, as it's only a shortish walk down to Respryn Bridge ❾, which is another popular swimming spot.

The attractive bridge is a five-arch medieval construction made from granite. The first bridge here was built in the 13th century; the oldest part of the present bridge is the central pointed arch, which dates back to the 15th century. Before the bridge there was a ford, and the 'res' of Respryn means ford, with the 'pryn' meaning crow - so 'Crow's Ford'. There was a chapel to St Martin here in the 12th century, which was common at fords during that time. The idea was that you would pray for safe passage, or if you were travelling in the opposite direction, give thanks for making the crossing safely.

The bridge linked the two major estates of Lanhydrock and Boconnoc and played a part in the English Civil War, when the former was Parliamentarian and the latter Royalist. King Charles rode over the bridge in 1644 when his army took Cornwall, but after the eventual Parliamentarian victory Lord Robartes planted an avenue of beech trees leading almost a mile from here up to Lanhydrock House to celebrate.

Cross the bridge and enter from the shingle beach for a refreshing swim under the canopy of leaves. At certain times of the year the sun-dappled waters are quite deep, and you can swim against the flow of the river without moving. Spring is an especially attractive time, when the nearby woodland is carpeted in bluebells – indeed the Lanhydrock woodlands are generally famed for bluebell displays.

The walk crosses the river one final time, over a wooden footbridge called Kathleen Bridge. The current structure was built in 1992 by the Royal Engineers, after its predecessor was swept away in floods. As you continue on your walk, look out for the evidence of tin streaming, because the banks and ditches hold clues to an industry that was common here in the late 1600s. Tin streams are formed by the erosion and build-up of loose tin-rich rocks in the bottom of river valleys. Layers of sand, gravel and peat then settle on top. The tinners removed these by hand, forming the banks and ditches you can still see today. They diverted streams so the water would wash away the lighter sands and silts, leaving the heavier prize of the tin-rich rocks.

If you still have the energy, seek out the potential final swimming spot near an island ⓬, before beginning the homeward walk through the semi-natural ancient woodland of Higginsmoor Wood. As you walk up the hill, look out for hornbeams, which are similar to beech trees, but have more sinewy trunks and smaller leaves with saw-toothed edges. As you follow the track towards Maudlin Wood, look out for the remains of Jacob's Quarry on your right. It was worked by Jacob Kestle and his son from the 1870s until the beginning of the First World War, providing stone for Cornish hedges and paths. There are also more remains of the old deer park wall to be seen in this area.

The walk back up to Lanhydrock House offers amazing views down across the valley where you have walked. The path takes you behind Garden Cottage and the old Lanhydrock kitchen garden on your right, then downhill along Garden Drive past some colourful rhododendrons, to reach the formal gardens of the main house and then past the gatehouse on your left. The house was the main setting for the 1996 film production of *Twelfth Night*, directed by Trevor Nunn and starring Helena Bonham Carter and Imogen Stubbs. Even if you haven't got the time to visit the interior, there are stunning views across the immaculate gardens from here. You will also pass The Avenue, the aforementioned magnificent beech-lined driveway **17**, which would take you back down to Respryn Bridge.

While much of the existing house is Victorian, some of the older areas date back much further. The estate originally belonged to the Augustinian priory of St Petroc in Bodmin, but following the dissolution of the monasteries it passed into private hands, and was bought by Sir Richard Robartes in 1620. While officially the Robartes family made their money through tin, according to one of the volunteers at the property they were actually known for loan sharking and served as the inspiration for the villainous Warleggan family in the *Poldark* novels. Construction of the house began in 1630, but Sir Richard was to die just four years into the build, leaving it to his son to complete in 1651. Following a devastating fire in 1881, the house was refurbished in the Victorian style you see today.

After centuries of sometimes illustrious and sometimes scandalous history, the Robartes family lost its heir at the Battle of Loos in France in the First World War, when he was killed trying to rescue a fellow soldier from no man's land. His younger brother became the 7th Viscount Clifden, but never married and gave the house and gardens to the National Trust in 1953. Even the title died out when the third brother died without a son in 1974. When *Love Island* contestant Ollie Williams boasted on the show that he was heir to the house and title, the National Trust was quick to point out that he was very much mistaken; he seems to have oversold his family, which does own estate lands that were not gifted over.

Apparently, the cute little thatched cottage you see when visiting the main house served as the

National Trust's first-ever tea room. Lanhydrock House also caused a storm in a tea cup back in 2018 when they accidentally created a Mother's Day cream tea advert that depicted a scone with jam dolloped on the cream – which is famously the Devon, not the Cornish, way of serving it. Outraged locals threatened to cancel their memberships, and over 300 complaints were received. Some over-the-top members described the mix-up as horrifying and said it made them 'feel sick'. The Trust apologised for the 'heinous mistake', adding that staff will wear #JamFirst badges to support 'a proper cream tea'.

If you have a little free time, you can take a stroll to visit the Victorian swimming pool, which today has been left to go back to nature and is a haven for local wildlife. You should be able to make out the changing room foundations and the old diving board stand, while in the waters you might spot ramshorn snails and palmate newts. Swimmers may be interested to know that the National Trust cafés serve 4.5 million cups of tea a year, which is enough to fill the traditional liquid measure of an Olympic swimming pool; thirsty walkers will be pleased to know there is a café waiting near the car park where we started.

1 In the car park, walk away from the road to the cricket field opposite. Turn left on the path that runs along the border of the cricket field, walking north-east with the cricket field on your right.
0.1 miles

2 At the end of the cricket field and the beginning of the wood turn right, following the orange sign that says 'Balance Bike Track'. Follow the track down through the woods.
0.2 miles

3 You reach a red gate. Turn left into the lane, which immediately comes to a T-junction with a track opposite, with a sign saying 'weak and narrow bridge'. Follow this track, and very shortly you reach a crossroads of tracks; turn right here following a sign for the 'National Cycle Network'. Follow the path down through the woods, ignoring cycle trail signs in a clearing on the right, then after that following the wooden posts

with yellow arrows. You reach a junction of paths with big stones; go straight on here.
0.8 miles

4 The path arrives at a road; cross this and go through another red gate with a sign instructing walkers to keep dogs on leads. Turn left and walk along with the river on your right.
0.3 miles

5 You reach a stone bridge; cross it and continue along the driveway with the black estate fencing past a water meadow on your right. Just before the railway bridge there is a small gate in the fence on the left. Go through here and bear right, walking upstream with the river on your left, to the viaduct.
0.2 miles

6 The swim spot is just the other side of the Bodmin Road Viaduct. After a swim, retrace your steps to the stone bridge in point 5. Here

you can go through a small gate just before the bridge on the left and swim below the bridge. After this, retrace your steps again back over the bridge for a short distance and start to follow the river downstream.
0.2 miles

7 Descend off the main path down to the river bank and walk along with the river on your left to reach the next swim spot on a double bend in the river.
0.2 miles

8 From the swim spot, continue walking along the bank with the river on your left, to Respryn Bridge.
0.5 miles

9 After a swim at Respryn Bridge, cross the bridge and continue through the wooden gate into the woods, with the river on your right, until you reach the wooden bridge.
0.3 miles

10 Cross Kathleen Bridge and continue, with the river now on your left.
0.2 miles

11 The river bends sharply to the left and there is a fork in the paths. Take the left fork, following the river.
0.1 miles

12 Your last swim spot is by the island. From here, retrace your steps to point 11 to take the other fork and follow the path gradually uphill.
0.2 miles

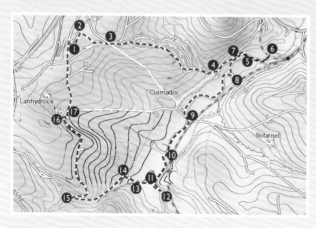

⓭ You reach a red gate; go through it and cross the small stone bridge over the stream, carrying on following the orange NT arrow on wooden post. Follow the path uphill, heading left at the fork.
0.1 miles

⓮ At the T-junction of paths, turn left following the orange NT arrow on a wooden post (if you turn right here you can cut through the estate back to the car park and shorten the walk). Follow the path uphill through the woods.
0.4 miles

⓯ You reach a T-junction with a wooden fingerpost for Lanhydrock House. Turn right here following the sign for the house, then keep going up and through the woods. The paths curves left and becomes a lane, where you pass Garden Cottage on the right.
0.7 miles

⓰ The lane comes out at the side of Lanhydrock House. Bear right around the front of the garden to get the full view of the house and park from the front.
0.1 miles

⓱ From the top of The Avenue in front of the house, follow the path north through the avenue of oak trees, past the Visitor Reception building on the right, across the road and back to the car park.
0.5 miles

Walk 25

LOOE ESTUARY ADVENTURE

A glorious adventure, walking up a gentle wooded estuary and swimming back down the smooth green river with the outgoing tide. Time the walk with high water, and bribe a friend to carry your stuff back, or drag a drybag-towfloat behind you.

INFORMATION

DISTANCE: 1.1 miles walking and 1.3 miles swimming, or 2.2 miles walking both ways
TIME: Allow 3 hours
MAP: OS Explorer 107 St Austell and Liskeard
START POINT: Millpool West Looe car park (SX 249 538, PL13 2FD).
END POINT: Millpool West Looe car park.
PUBLIC TRANSPORT: Bus routes 72 from Plymouth, 73 from Liskeard, 428 from St Austell and 481 from Polruan serve Looe. The Looe branch line from Liskeard is one of the prettiest in the country. The station is 0.7 miles from the start (greatscenicrailways.co.uk).
SWIMMING: West Looe River from Watergate (SX 234 546) down to the slipway in the car park (SX 248 538), Hannafore Beach (SX 257 524).
PLACES OF INTEREST: The Old Sardine Factory, Looe Island.
REFRESHMENTS: The century-old Martin's Dairy Bakery and Tea Rooms is near the station in East Looe, and does great pasties (01503 262505, PL13 1HH). The Island View Café looks out to sea (07443 460874, PL13 2DJ).
EASIER ACCESS: Swim from the car park at high water. Get dropped off at East Looe Beach (SX 256 531); no parking right by the beach, but a sand wheelchair is available.
NEARBY SWIM SPOTS: Portnadler Bay is a scenic, quiet beach further down the coast, west of Hannafore. Walk to it along the coast path or from the National Trust car park at Hendersick. Talland Bay has charming twin beaches.

ooe is a delightful and bustling little town, nestled on the banks of the river that bears its name. There are two branches, the West Looe and the East Looe Rivers, which form a confluence in the town and flow out to sea past all manner of quays, jetties and slipways. Most distinctive is the Banjo Pier, its rounded end designed to stop the harbour silting up. The Cornish poet and naturalist Geoffrey Grigson was born near West Looe and wrote of the river: "Two streams come down two deep valleys to the tidal water. Five minutes' walk to the sea, the two valleys merge into one…. no road penetrates right up the valley parallel to the little trout, sea trout, salmon, dipper and kingfisher and sandpiper river, which runs down under the alders and over stones of red-veined quartz to the wider tidal portions above the sea."

East Looe and West Looe, on opposite sides of the river, have historically been separate towns, with their own mayors and governance. The east is the busier side, more geared to tourism; the west has traditionally been much quieter, though the conversion of an old sardine factory into a museum and restaurant in 2018 is bringing more visitors to this side of the river.

The town is a working fishing port with around 50 commercial boats, and its history as a trading port can be traced back to pre-medieval times. Back then it exported tin, arsenic and granite, as well as being home to the boatbuilding and fishing industries. Records show that in 1347 the town provided 20 ships to supply the famous siege of Calais during the Hundred Years War.

KILMINORTH WOODS
Local Nature Reserve

Jack The Giant
Having Nothing To Do
Built A Hedge
From Lerryn To Looe

The walk starts in an enormous car park at the bottom of the West Looe River, just before the confluence. You have the river beside you pretty much all the time on this walk, so it's very difficult to get lost. To start, you walk past the slipway at the western end of the car park before heading into the woods.

This is Kilminorth Wood ❷, known locally as the 'Lungs of Looe'. You will walk under a variety of trees including oak, beech, sycamore, holly and rowan, and the area is classed as ancient woodland. It's home to lots of wildlife including foxes, badgers and roe deer, as well as flora such as bluebells, violets, wood sorrel and wood anemones.

The path stays close to the water most of the time, giving enticing glimpses of the beautiful estuary. At the point where the river bends sharply to the left, you walk over an ancient earthwork called the Giant's Hedge, although there's nothing to tell you it's there apart from the way the ground rises. According to the South West Coast Path Association, it's part of a large earthwork from the 6th century between the Looe and Fowey estuaries. It was originally 9 miles long, and thought to have been built by a local chieftain to defend his territory. Only parts of it remain, one of which is here in Kilminorth Wood.

The walk emerges at the hamlet of Watergate ❸, where the legend of the Giant's Hedge is recorded in a poem embossed on a large rock you will see by the river:

> *Jack the Giant having nothing to do,*
> *Built a hedge from Lerryn to Looe.*

If you are swimming, get into the water here. The swim is best done at high water on a spring tide, when there will be the maximum water possible in the river; start swimming about an hour after high water to get the best push. On a neap tide you may have to wade from time to time, but

this is all part of the fun too. Also, this is a great river for an adventure swim, because it is very safe and there are lots of get-out points; if you tire, you can just get out and walk.

It truly is a magical swim. There is no evidence of human presence along the river at all, apart from the odd fellow swimmer, kayaker or paddleboarder. The trees spread up the banks on either side, and it feels timeless. You could be swimming in medieval times or even in prehistory, and the scene would not look much different. Enjoy the smooth, green silky water and look out for birdlife as you swim; if you are lucky you might spot a kingfisher fly past like a flash of blue electricity. Other birds you are likely to see include herons, egrets, curlews and Canada geese.

The swim finishes at the slipway at the car park, where it is easy to get out and you will have the satisfaction of having swum back to where you started.

Afterwards, you can head to the beach for a contrasting sea swim. East Looe Beach is lovely, but our favourite is Hannafore, which is pebbly with a reef and clear water, rockpools and many different types of shells. It is also on the western side of the town, about a mile away, so if you have the energy you can walk from the car park. Otherwise it is a short drive on a very scenic route along the river and quayside and around the headland to the beach.

The best thing about the beach is the view across to Looe Island, also known as St George's Island. Once a religious site and then a convenient place for smugglers to hide their contraband, in the early 1960s it was bought by sisters Evelyn and Babs Atkins, who lived there for 40 years. Evelyn wrote two books about it all, called *We Bought An Island* and *Tales from our Cornish Island*. She describes her first visit to the island: "We had stepped into another world. We were in time to see the most spectacular sunset from the bridge. The lichen-covered rocks below us and the dramatic cliffs of the southern coastline glowed gold, purple and wondrous shades of rose in the rays of the setting sun far out into the Atlantic." The sisters left the island to the Cornwall Wildlife Trust, and since 2004 it has been a nature reserve and can be visited on trips organised by the Trust.

DIRECTIONS

1 From the car park, walk past the slipway on your right and head towards the woods with the river on your right.
0.1 miles

2 You reach a wooden sign post saying 'Riverside and Watergate' with a yellow, blue and red dot. Shortly after that there is a wooden five-bar gate saying 'Kilminorth Woods'. Simply follow the path through the woods, with the river on your right, until you reach the road at Watergate.
1 mile

3 At Watergate, descend right to the water and swim back. Walkers can retrace their steps back to the start.
1.3 miles swimming,
1.1 miles walking

4 Exit the water at the slipway in the car park.

Walk 26

MINIONS TO GOLDIGGINS QUARRY CIRCULAR

A fascinating walk across the moors, taking in thousands of years of history and a swim in a legendary spring-fed quarry lake.

INFORMATION

DISTANCE: 4 miles
TIME: 3–4 hours depending on picnicking time
MAP: OS Explorer 109 Bodmin Moor
START POINT: Minions Heritage Centre car park (SX 262 713, PL14 5LL).
END POINT: Minions Heritage Centre car park.
PUBLIC TRANSPORT: Bus route 174 from Liskeard station stops in Upton Cross, 1.3-mile walk from the car park.
SWIMMING: The Pony Pool (SX 255 720), Goldiggins Quarry (SX 249 723)
PLACES OF INTEREST: Minions Heritage Centre, Rillaton Barrow, the Cheesewring, the Pipers, the Hurlers.
REFRESHMENTS: Minions Shop & Tearooms is a great place to enjoy Kelly's ice-cream or Cornish pasties, and it's also licensed, should you fancy a Cornish cider or local ale (01579 228652, PL14 5LE). The family-run Cheesewring Hotel is the highest pub in Cornwall (01579 362321, PL14 5LE).
EASIER ACCESS: There is a fairly flat track from the Hurlers car park west of Minions straight up to Goldiggins Quarry.
NEARBY SWIM SPOTS: Golitha Falls on the River Fowey has dipping pools; Dozmary Pool is a little shallow, but famed for its links with Arthurian legend and the Faustian figure of Jan Tregeagle; it is worth checking out just because of its history.

his part of Cornwall is all about what lies beneath. The history here is summed up by Daphne du Maurier in her book *Vanishing Cornwall* in 1967: "The underworld that promised immortality held its treasures too, so that Cornishmen from the beginning, have always dug for wealth. They were, are, tinners, copper-seekers, quarriers, slate-breakers, clay-workers, farmers; an earthy people with an earthy knowledge, the word earthy used not as a slight but as a salutation."

Our walk begins in the village of Minions ❶, which can be found on the eastern flank of Bodmin Moor. It lays claim to being the highest village in Cornwall, with most of the village more than 300 metres above sea level. The name has nothing to do with the little yellow henchmen from *Despicable Me*, but is derived from the Cornish name Menyon, meaning stones. And that's rather apt, because the landscape here is all about stones, including quarries, standing stones, tors, Bronze Age stone circles and burial mounds. Even our swim is in a spring-fed quarry lake, which is quite legendary among wild swimmers.

The village itself was constructed between 1863 and 1880 to support the mining and quarrying industry, the evidence of which can been seen all around you from the car park. Tin and copper mining took place here up till 1914, when the Prince of Wales shaft closed. A railway line was built for the industry, and both metals from the mines and granite from the quarries were transported to Liskeard and on to Looe for shipping.

While the tracks have gone, we will still be following the old railway routes on the first part of the walk. You won't be able to miss Caradon Hill, with a television transmission mast on its summit. The South Caradon Mine once extracted copper south-west of the transmitter, while on the western flank of the hill, a quarry has recently started cutting granite again.

Above the car park you will see one of the former engine houses of the South Phoenix Mine, which is now the Minions Heritage Centre and open over the summer months. The walk heads off to the right of the building and follows the former railway track. It's worth taking a diversion off to the left to see a tumulus called the Rillaton Barrow ❸. It doesn't look spectacular – it's just a medium-sized mound – but it has some amazing history. A gold cup dating back to the Bronze Age was discovered here, and was among finds sent as a Duchy Treasure Trove to King William IV. It was apparently used to store collar studs on the royal dressing table, but after the death of King George V in 1936 the importance of the cup was appreciated, and it is now in the British Museum; a replica can be seen in the Royal Cornwall Museum in Truro.

A legend associated with the cup is that the Rillaton Barrow is said to be haunted by the spirit of a druid priest, who would offer thirsty travellers a drink from a bottomless cup. One night a traveller threw the cup's contents at the ghost in frustration and was later found dead in a ravine.

It's actually possible to see inside the burial mound with the use of a torch; there is a stone-lined chamber on the side of it, which is an ancient cist or burial place. Not many of these survive, so take a look, although do watch out for ghostly druids and any tempting treats they may offer.

The views from the burial mound are impressive, with the chimneys of former mines in the distance resembling the hours on an over-sized clock. You will also be able to see our next destination, the Cheesewring ❻, a curious natural granite formation overlooking a quarry of the same name. It resembles a giant version of the stacks of pebbles

that some people construct on beaches. The name comes from a type of press used to extract liquid either from cheese or from apples for cider – the apple pulp left behind was also known as cheese. These traditional presses can still be seen occasionally today, and do indeed resemble the stones.

Although it looks manmade, the tor is actually a natural formation, carved by the weathering of layers of granite slabs over thousands of years. With larger slabs balancing on top of smaller slabs, it looks like the whole thing could fall over at any minute.

In his 1861 book *Rambles Beyond Railways*, Wilkie Collins wrote: "If a man dreams of a great pile of stones in a nightmare, he would dream of such a pile as the Cheesewring. All the heaviest and largest of the seven thick slabs of which it is composed are at the top; all the lightest and smallest at the bottom. It rises perpendicularly to a height of thirty-two feet, without lateral support of any kind. The fifth and sixth rocks are of immense size and thickness, and overhang fearfully all-round the four lower rocks which support them. All are perfectly irregular; the projections of one do not fit into the interstices of another; they are heaped up loosely in their extraordinary top-heavy form on slanting ground, half way down a steep hill."

The tor has been a popular tourist attraction for hundreds of years, and there are a couple of legends attached to it. Apparently, the top stone magically spins around three times whenever it hears a cockerel crow, which would definitely be worth getting up early for! Another tale says it was created during a contest between a giant and an early Christian saint. According to the legend, the giants were angry that their land was being invaded by Christian missionaries, so Uther, one of the largest, challenged the weedy-looking St Tue to a rock-throwing contest. If the giant won, the saints

would have to leave Cornwall, while if the saint won, the giants would have to convert to Christianity. Uther first threw a small rock onto the top of Stowe's Hill. After praying, Tue found that he could easily pick up a huge slab of stone and throw it. They took turns throwing their stones, which landed in perfect piles. Eventually, the score was 12 stones each and it was Uther's turn. He threw, but his stone rolled down the hill. Tue picked it up, and an angel took it from his hands and carried it to the top of the pile of rocks. Realising that he was defeated, Uther conceded, and he and most of the other giants converted to Christianity.

A walk up to the tor is well worth it, offering stunning views across the moors. You will be able to see ruined engine houses off to the east, and our swim spots at the Pony Pool ❼ and Golddiggins – or Gold Diggings – Quarry ❾ as you turn around to the west. The Cheesewring sits within the massive stone wall of a Neolithic enclosure called

Stowe's Pound, sharing the summit with over 100 house platforms. At the base of the tor, look out for more recent habitation: a small cave-like opening in a pile of rocks with the inscription 'D Gumb 1735' carved above it. This what remains of a larger construction where local stonemason Daniel Gumb lived, possibly with his wife and children, and there are other carvings on the roof.

According to the story, he disliked the idea of paying taxes so much, he decided to live in the cave he created from discarded blocks of granite from the quarry. He did have another motivation for living on the moor though: he was a mathematician and a stargazer, with the cave being an observatory on one of the highest points in Cornwall. He died in 1776, and you can still see several gravestones that were carved by him in the churchyard at Linkinhorne, including his own.

The walk continues past the Pony Pool, which as the name suggests is a small lake the animals drink from. When we were there, a herd of cattle were enjoying the cool waters. People do swim here, and it has a sandy beach that children will enjoy, as well as a small waterfall at certain times of the year. However, the real goal of Goldiggins Quarry is so close that you may want to save yourself for this stunning swim spot. Historically known as Swit Quarry, it was once mined for both granite and beryl but to the best of our knowledge no gold has ever been found here; the strange name might come from the hopes of profit, or the colour of the beryl. It's a stunning spot that looks like a natural amphitheatre, with high cliffs giving way to grassy banks and clear emerald waters.

There are a couple of smaller pools in the quarry, but it is in the enchanted waters of the main quarry lake that you'll want to bathe. There are also plenty of ledges above the deep waters where youngsters enjoy fulfilling a natural rite of passage by jumping in – obviously, check the depth of the water before throwing yourself from any height. The Scottish band Travis filmed the video for *Why Does it Always Rain on Me?* here, and it's worth looking it up on the web to see lead singer Fran Healy jump into the quarry from the highest point, wearing a kilt. The song became an international hit and gained legendary status when they performed it at the Glastonbury Festival in 1999 on a bright, sunny day: it began to rain as the first line was sung.

The quarry also makes a great spot for a picnic, and sadly this means it has become a hot spot for littering, which puts the future access to wild swimming there at risk. Perhaps you could take a spare rubbish bag on this walk, to pick up some extra litter and help us share the message that wild swimmers are very proactive when it comes to protecting the environment. There are rubbish bins at the car park, so it's not too far to carry anything with you.

It's a really scenic walk back to the car park with plenty of time to take in the distant views of old buildings and chimneys from the area's industrial past. There are also a couple of prehistoric treats in store for you before the end. If you like, you can search out the fallen stones of Craddock Moor Circle ❿, which lies amid a scattering of cairns and stone rows. Later you will see two standing stones known as the Pipers ⓫ and then three stone circles known as the Hurlers. The two outer stone circles are round while the large one in the middle is slightly elliptical. The name Hurlers comes from a legend that a group of men were turned to stone while playing Cornish hurling on a Sunday. The Pipers are supposed to be the figures of two men who played music on the Sabbath and suffered the same fate. Seth Lakeman wrote a 2008 song about the Hurlers, but we don't know if he ever dared perform it on a Sunday – especially here.

The crossroads near the Hurlers features several times in the television series *Poldark*, when characters are riding on horseback between Nampara and Trenwith; remarkably, the sea was matted into the background. Hollywood has also used this area for locations in films including *The Kid Who Would Be King*, about a young boy who finds King Arthur's legendary sword Excalibur, and *Miss Peregrine's Home for Peculiar Children* directed by Tim Burton. In 2015 a road sign was erected outside the village featuring the little yellow characters as part of the publicity for the upcoming *Minions* movie, paid for by Universal Studios and featuring the message 'Please Drive Carefully'. Ironically, while it caused a big boost in tourism, it was eventually removed for safety reasons, as families were posing in the road next to the sign for photographs.

1 From the car park, follow the fingerpost saying 'The Cheesewring' towards and then to the right of the old mine ruin, now the Minions Heritage Centre. Follow the track as it bends to the right past a stone wall and some trees, then bears left.
0.5 miles

2 A small, higher path starts to the left and parallel to the main track. About 200 metres along this, turn left away from the main track and follow a faint path to the burial mound.
0.1 miles

3 From Rillaton Barrow, head back to the main track and continue with the Cheesewring ahead in the distance. You will see the remains of the old granite railway forking left. Follow it past some old mine shafts on your left, and stay on the track as it bears left around the quarry.
0.4 miles

4 You reach a junction with two paths to the right like a skewed crossroads, with the Cheesewring up and to your right; take the second path, around the hill.
0.1 miles

5 Turn right by a hawthorn tree to follow a winding path up to the summit.
0.1 miles

6 From the Cheesewring, retrace your steps back to the junction with the track, and turn right to follow it until you see fenced-off mine shafts on your left. Turn left between the mine shafts to reach the Pony Pool.
0.4 miles

7 From the Pony Pool, retrace your steps to the track, turn left and keep on the main track as it bears left, ignoring the first turn to the right. Follow the path uphill with the Pony Pool on your left.
0.3 miles

8 At the brow of the hill you reach a sort of staggered crossroads. Take the first right, which is the lower track, and follow it to the quarry.
0.4 miles

9 From Goldiggins Quarry, do not return on the path you came in on but follow the main track. Shortly after the big tyre in the middle of the track, the track bends to the left. At this point you can turn right off the main track and walk down to visit a stone circle.
0.4 miles

10 From Craddock Moor circle, rejoin the main track and continue to retrace your steps until you reach point 8 again. Turn right here and follow the main track back towards the village.
0.7 miles

11 At the Pipers standing stones on the left turn, left off the path to the Hurlers stone circles visible on the skyline. From the Hurlers you can see the Heritage Centre from the start, and walk across the moor to it and the car park.
0.4 miles

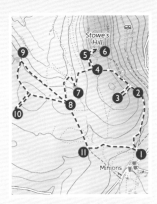

Walk 27

PORTWRINKLE AND SHEVIOCK CIRCULAR

A strenuous walk with magnificent views, between a fort, an old smugglers' village and an ancient ferry crossing on a tidal river. The walk needs to be timed so as to reach the first swim spot about an hour before high tide, and check the firing times at Tregantle.

INFORMATION

DISTANCE: 8 miles
TIME: 6 hours
FIRING TIMES: To Check firing times at Tregantle Fort see www.gov.uk/government/publications/tregantle-firing-notice
MAP: OS Explorer 108 Lower Tamar Valley and Plymouth
START POINT: Viewpoint parking layby at B3246 (SX 389 533, PL11 3AY.
END POINT: Parking layby at viewpoint.
PUBLIC TRANSPORT: Bus routes 70B between Plymouth and Millbrook and 75 between Torpoint and Liskeard both call at Portwrinkle and Sheviock.
SWIMMING: Finnygook Beach (SX 359 538), Hoodny Cove (SX 354 538), Lynher River (SX 378 557).
PLACES OF INTEREST: Tregantle Fort, St Mary's Church.
REFRESHMENTS: The Jolly Roger Café is on the beach at Portwrinkle (01503 230655, PL11 3BT). The Finnygook Inn in Crafthole has great views down to the River Lynher and beyond (01503 230338, PL11 3BQ).
EASIER ACCESS: You can park next to the beach at Portwrinkle. There is parking by the River Lynher at Wacker Quay just off the A374, from where you can swim at high tide.
NEARBY SWIM SPOTS: The twin villages of Kingsand and Cawsand just over Rame Head are very popular with swimmers, as they are sheltered and the water is usually calm. Another lovely spot on the headland is Queen Adelaide's Grotto at Penlee Point, where you can walk down and swim on a small beach.

The walk starts by the rather spectacular Tregantle Fort ❷, a Victorian military base made more exciting by the fact it is still in use today. When there is live firing you must follow an alternative route for the first part of the walk; flags will be flying, or you can check firing times on the government website (see Information). While you're planning, check the tide times, and set off on the walk about two hours before high tide.

The fort was built between 1858 and 1865 in response to Napoleon's military might. Until then, Britain had been sitting comfortably as the world's major naval force, but when Napoleon came along all that changed and there was the threat of invasion. The government of Lord Palmerston ordered the construction of a whole series of forts and batteries along the British coast. They became known as Palmerston's Follies because by the time they were finished the military threat had passed.

The fort is very imposing and roughly hexagonal in shape. The path runs right past it, and although you can't go inside, you do get a sense of the times in which it was built. Today it is used by all three armed forces for training, not without incident; in 2020 a Royal Marine died during a training exercise off the beach below the fort.

You pass various firing ranges and a plethora of official notices, and it feels quite surreal walking through a military base in such a spectacular position on the cliffs. As you pass the fort and walk towards Portwrinkle the views are magnificent. Just after you turn from the base on the footpath, you are at a high point from where you can see for miles on a clear day. Look around from Kit Hill to Brent Tor, the St Germans or Lynher River (which you will be visiting later) and the city of Plymouth. If you turn back, you can see Rame Head with its medieval chapel on top, to the other side of the fort. The path hugs the coast and then clips the edge of a golf course (be alert for flying golf balls) and then winds down to the village of Portwrinkle.

As the path descends towards the village you will see a striking grey stone mansion to your right. This was the Whitsand Bay Hotel, which after welcoming guests for over a hundred years was put up for sale in 2018 with planning permission to be converted into flats. Opposite, on the seaward side of the road, is another astonishing building called Serpentine, an oval modern house with a flat sedum roof. Billed as an 'eco holiday home', it has an entire curved wall of glass facing out to sea, and can be rented for rather a lot of money. Between them, the two illustrate how much British holidays have changed.

The village is strung along the coast road, and its history is all about fishing and smuggling. In the 17th century pilchard fishing was the main industry, and you can still see the fish cellars that were built then just before the harbour, now converted into homes. At the same time, smuggling was rife, and the most notorious smuggler in the village was Silas Finn, whose name lives on at Finnygook Beach and the nearby Finnygook Inn.

He regularly disguised himself as a woman to escape capture, but it all went wrong for him one night when he was caught red-handed. Facing the gallows, he decided to do a deal with customs and excise. In exchange for his life, he waved a light from the cliffs above the village – the usual signal

that the coast was clear and it was safe to bring the contraband ashore – luring in fellow smugglers who were arrested and dealt with. It is said that his ghost (the 'gook' in Finnygook) haunts the cliffs, full of remorse at the betrayal of his friends.

The village has several swim spots. The first is Finnygook Beach ❹, in front of Serpentine. It has an extensive reef that is perfect for snorkelling at high tide, and rockpooling at low. Then you reach the village's diminutive harbour ❺, which is the perfect swimming pool at high tide, especially when the sea is rough. Next to that is Hoodny Cove. On a calm day, it is wonderful to swim at high tide from Finnygook Beach over the reef to Hoodny Cove (or the other way round). Some locals like to swim the mile between Portwrinkle and the Long Stone, a large rock off the headland further west down the beach.

After your swim, it's time to head inland, up the lane to the village of Crafthole ❻. This was also allegedly part of the smuggling industry, with booty being stored in a room at the Methodist chapel in the 19th century. You then follow a footpath down through a beautiful wooded valley along a stream, passing an old reservoir that is now a fishing lake. You reach a main road and walk along it for a short distance to Sheviock, where the well-preserved medieval parish church of St Mary's ❾ is one of the few in Cornwall to have a spire.

From here you follow a public footpath called George's Lane, which is an ancient track through woods, eventually leading to what used to be an old ferry crossing over to Erth Hill on the other side ⓫. It is not known when the ferry ceased operating (cars led to the demise of the nearby Antony Passage ferry in the 1950s) but there are the remains of a building on the other side, which could have been part of the ferry set-up. There was apparently also a quay here in the 18th century.

This tidal river is known as the St Germans River or Lynher River. The Victorian writer, Wilkie Collins, describes being rowed up to St Germans from Saltash on the first night of his walking tour of Cornwall in 1851: "… the arm of the sea, up which we were proceeding, was in many places more than half a mile across; on the broad, smooth surface of the stream the moonlight lay fair and unruffled; the woods clothing the hills on each side, grew down to the water's edge, and were darkly reflected, all along, in solemn winding shapes. Sometimes we passed an old ship, rotten and mastless, anchored solitary, midway between land and land. Sometimes we saw, afar off, a light in a fisherman's cottage among the trees; but we met no boats, saw no living beings, heard no voices on our lonely way."

This is a beautifully quiet swim spot, which dries out at low water. It is a great place to see wading birds including egrets and spoonbills, and you may even spot a kingfisher if you're lucky. If you swim out into the middle you can look up river towards St Germans and the two distinctive viaducts that carry the train line into Cornwall. After your swim it's a winding walk back through some tiny hamlets back to the start.

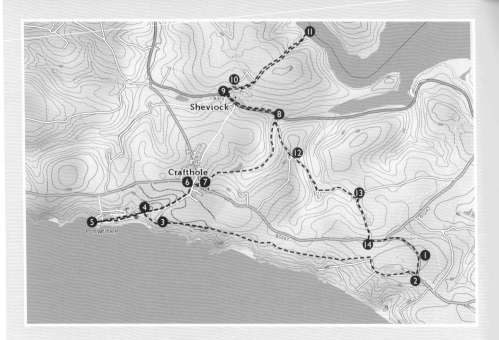

There are two routes for the start of this walk, depending on whether flags are flying. Flying flags indicate that there is firing underway at the fort.

NO FIRING ROUTE

❶ If flags are not flying, turn left along the road with the fort on your right.
0.1 miles

❷ Go into the fort entrance at the sign on the bend saying 'Tregantle Fort and Ranges'. Head towards the main building and turn left at a big sign saying 'slow troops marching'. Follow the road, which bends right and passes by

the fort on your right and D range on your left. Continue on the road up the hill, following the sign with the acorn and arrow, and pass F range on your left. Just after F range and the MOD red firing range signs, turn right to follow the public footpath. Go through the wooden kissing gate and turn left onto the coast path. Follow the path with the sea on your left all the way to the golf course.
1.8 miles

FIRING ROUTE

❶ If flags are flying, turn right and walk west along the road with the fort on your left. Turn left through a wooden gate with an acorn and

follow the path down along the hedge on your left and through another field to join the coast path. Turn right, walking with the sea on your left all the way to the golf course.
1.8 miles

❸ You reach a wooden sign in the golf course with yellow arrows pointing straight on and right. Go straight on here, continuing the hug the coast, until the path joins with the coast road. Turn left here and walk along the road into Portwrinkle to the café and parking area. Just before the café is a path down to your first swim spot.
0.2 miles

4 From Finnygook Beach you could swim on westwards to the next stop. Otherwise retrace your steps up the path to the road, and turn left past the café and parking area along the seafront. Head left past the old fish cellars where the road bends right.
0.3 miles

5 Descend to the little harbour (or Hoodny Cove next to it) for a swim. After, retrace your steps past the parking area and café and follow the road up out of the village until you get to Crafthole.
0.7 miles

6 At the crossroads in Crafthole, turn right following signs for Millbrook and Torpoint, and then at the mini-roundabout turn sharp left for Sheviock.
0.1 miles

7 Take the public footpath very shortly on the right, just after the stone house. Follow it down past the old reservoir on the left until

you get to a small lane. Turn left into the lane.
0.8 miles

8 At the main road turn left and walk until you reach the village of Sheviock.
0.4 miles

9 Just past St Mary's church turn right into George's Lane and follow it.
0.1 miles

10 At a fork with some slate house signs including 'The Keep' and 'Linden Cottage', take the left fork and follow the path down to the river, past farm buildings on the left and then through a field and down through woods.
0.6 miles

11 Have a swim and then retrace your steps back to point 8. Turn right off the main road up the narrow lane (passing the path you walked down before) and walk up the hill.
1.3 miles

12 Just past a house with a blue window you arrive at a T-junction. Turn left here. Follow the lane around the converted barn with the rounded corner, down past some ornamental lakes on your left and back up the hill.
0.6 miles

13 You reach a fork with a house called 1, Blerrick Farm Cottages on your left. Turn right here and walk up the lane.
0.3 miles

14 At the main coast road, turn left and follow the road past the turning for Torpoint and Antony, back to the layby car park.
0.4 miles

SLOW TROOPS MARCHING SPEED LIMIT 10MPH

Walk 28

COTEHELE AND TAMAR SWOOSH

An adventurous walk and tidal swim along the River Tamar, the border between Cornwall and Devon, passing reminders of centuries of farming and industrial change.

bit of advance planning is needed for part of today's escapade, as you will be finishing it by swimming a mile down the river from Calstock to Cotehele Quay with the outgoing tide. Either take a drybag-towfloat to carry your clothes back with you, or enlist a walking friend who can take it. You can twist their arm by explaining that they will also be rewarded with a riverside walk through a woodland that provides stunning valley views and even a secret chapel to explore. If that fails, there's a café at the end, so you can bribe them with the promise of delicious cake.

You will also need to work with the tides, as you want to reach Calstock about an hour after high tide to take advantage of the tidal assistance that makes the swim so much fun. Of course, swimming a mile may not be your cup of tea, even with the help of the tide, in which case you can have a lovely dip or two at Calstock or at Cotehele.

The walk starts down at the historic Cotehele Quay ❶, part of the estate owned by the National Trust. Back in the 19th century, the quay would have been bustling with vessels loading and unloading cargo that travelled between here and Plymouth along the Tamar. Smaller boats carried the produce down to Devonport market to be sold on. Meanwhile, crowded paddle steamers transported curious tourists to get a glimpse of the colourful orchards for which the area was famed.

The lime kilns you see close to the car park are also connected to the thriving produce industry. Coal from Bristol and limestone from Plymouth were bought upriver to produce lime, which was

INFORMATION

DISTANCE: 4.5 miles
TIME: Allow 5 hours
MAP: OS Explorer 108 Lower Tamar Valley and Plymouth
START POINT: Cotehele Quay. National Trust car park (SX 424 681, PL12 6TA).
END POINT: Cotehele Quay National Trust car park.
PUBLIC TRANSPORT: Bus routes 79/79A from Tavistock or Callington serve Calstock Quay. Or take the Tamar Valley Line from Plymouth to Calstock Station, start the swim from here and walk back afterwards.
SWIMMING: From the slipway in Calstock (SX 436 685) to Cotehele Quay (SX 424 681).
PLACES OF INTEREST: Cotehele Quay, Discovery Centre, the Mill, Prospect Tower, ruined buildings in Danescombe Valley, Calstock, Chapel-in-the-Wood.
REFRESHMENTS: The Edgcumbe on Cotehele Quay (National Trust) is great for a light lunch or cream tea (01579 352717, PL12 6TA). Their Kiosk also serves drinks, cakes and ice-creams. The Boot Inn in Calstock is a 17th-century village inn that has a more relaxed area where dogs are welcome, as well as a posher gastro pub (01822 481589, PL18 9RN).
EASIER ACCESS: Slipway at Calstock and steps or slipways at Cotehele Quay are close to parking (can be muddy).
NEARBY SWIM SPOTS: Downderry is a sheltered sand and shingle beach. The twin villages of Kingsand and Cawsands have pebbly beaches to swim from.

199

ideal for fertilising the market gardens where apples, strawberries and cherries were grown.

A great way of learning more, either before or after your swim walk, is to pop into the Discovery Centre on the quay, which tells the story of the Tamar Valley. Entry is free, and there are models of the historic boats and ships that worked the river, as well as tableaux that show how the quay with its boat yard and lime kilns looked in its heyday.

You will also learn about the project to restore Shamrock, a 19-metre traditional Tamar sailing barge that can be seen outside the Discovery Centre. She was launched in 1899 to haul coal, limestone, sand, fertiliser and manure up and down the river. At the time of writing, she was undergoing a programme of major repairs to return her to the river where she belongs.

Today guided canoe trips leave from the slipways, while you will also spot gig rowers and paddleboarders enjoying the river that separates Devon from Cornwall. According to Cornish folklore, the other side of the Tamar was where the devil lived. Indeed, one traditional boast was

that the devil would never cross the river for fear of ending up as a pasty filling. The story is told in the folk song *Fish and Tin and Copper*, which dates back hundreds of years and relates how the devil crosses the border and peers in through the window of a rustic cottage:

> *And in the kitchen might be seen*
> *A dame with knife in hand,*
> *Who cut and slashed and chopped, I ween*
> *To make a pasty grand.*
> *"Good Mornin', Missus, what is that?"*
> *"Of all sorts, is a daub.*
> *'Tis beef and mutton, pork and fat,*
> *Potatoes, leeks, and squab."*
> *"A Cornish pasty, sure", says she,*
> *"And if thou doesn't mind,*
> *I soon shall start to cut up thee*
> *And put ye in, you'll find!"*
> *In fear he turned and straight did flee*
> *Across the Tamar green*
> *And since that day in Cornwall*
> *He has never more been seen!*

The walk begins by turning away from the Tamar and following the Morden Stream up into the woods to the weir, with a diversion to Cotehele Mill ❹. The mill ground grain that had been bought up the river from Plymouth, and also powered a sawmill and generated electricity. Today, the restored mill produces flour (grinding can be seen on Tuesdays and Thursdays) for the restaurant to use, as well as for general sale to the public. There are also artisan craft workshops where you can watch a furniture maker and a potter at work, as well as re-creations of a saddler's, a wheelwright's and a blacksmith's shop.

You then retrace your steps to the main path through the woods, before continuing along a permissive path provided by the landowner to fill in the final piece in a circular route from Cotehele Quay. The field is managed to benefit nature conservation, while the avenue of cherry trees ❼ has been created to replicate the planting shown on a map from 1880. This area was known for fruit growing in the past; Newton Farm was central to this and also linked to the Edgcumbe family of Cotehele.

The walk soon takes you down a very steep field towards the wooded river valley. Off to the right you will be able to see Prospect Tower, a folly that was built around 1789 by the 2nd Earl of Mount Edgcumbe in celebration of the royal visit of King George III. The three-sided tower is 18 metres high, with mostly 'blind' windows. The National Trust renovated it in 1947 and replaced the spiral staircase to allow visitors to climb to the top.

When you reach Danescombe valley ⓬, you will spot old buildings and ruins that give a clue to the industries that once operated from here. These include the former Danescombe Sawmill as well as 19th-century mines that once extracted tin, copper and arsenic (which protected cotton against the boll weevil). If you were to walk further up the valley you would also spot a ruined paper mill that used to produce brown paper, pasteboard and millboard, used primarily for book covers. The mill later produced paper to wrap the soft fruits that left the area via Plymouth.

Further down the path, don't miss a mini cottage industry of today in the form of Danescombe Pottery. It was set up in 1993 by Swedish-born potter Ann-Mari Hopkins and sells distinctive blue and brown glazed items inspired by the nearby river. If you want to buy something you leave money in an envelope and post it through the door of the cottage next door.

The walk then joins the road to Calstock ⓭, a lane passing old engine houses, boat yards and

lovely riverside properties. Our favourite is the striking Danescombe Valley House, a stunning Grade-II-listed Victorian house on the bend in the river, which dates from the 1850s. Originally built as a fishing lodge for the Ashburton family, it then operated as a small hotel from the late 1800s till 1999. Today it's a private family home, which we are saving our pennies to buy. The magnificent 12 arches of the Calstock Viaduct soon come into view; these are where adventurous swimmers will be getting in the water.

The viaduct was built in 1907 and is nearly 40 metres high. Today it carries the Tamar Valley line, which runs from Plymouth to Gunnislake, but in the past it carried minerals from the nearby mines. A 15-ton wagon lift against one of the viaduct piers would hoist a wagon of ore up to the top to continue its journey by rail, but this was dismantled and sold for scrap in 1934.

The village itself is well worth a visit, with a couple of pubs and a lively arts scene. This includes a contemporary art gallery and Calstock Arts, a community centre that you pass on your left as you enter the village – look for the amazing window overlooking the river. It's built in a converted chapel and hosts music, film, comedy, talks and exhibitions.

Enter the water from the public slipway above the viaduct, but do be careful as unfortunately it's called a slipway for a reason. If you have got your timing right, your swim should be delightfully water-assisted as you head towards the viaduct. We think it is vital that you float on your back as you go under it. We waved at several friendly people in riverside properties as we 'swooshed' down the river, travelling at such a speed that the walkers were having trouble keeping up with us on the banks. In between slaloming in and out around the moored boats, you might even fancy visiting 'England' by crossing to the reeded banks on the far side of the river. Don't forget your passport!

Soon you will be at the bend in the river by Dane-scombe Valley House and heading down through an unspoilt stretch that feels like you are exploring the Amazon – although without the piranhas and alligators. Our laughter could be heard echoing down the river valley, but our walkers were having fun too. They returned via the hidden Chapel-in-the-Wood **17** high up in the woods. It marks the spot where Richard Edgcumbe made a narrow escape from royal soldiers in 1483, a story straight out of an Alexandre Dumas-style adventure.

He was part of a rebellion against Richard III and was being pursued through the woods by the king's men. In a moment of inspiration, he threw his hat in the river and hid in the trees. His enemies spotted the floating hat and presumed he had drowned while trying to cross the river. This allowed Richard to escape to exile in Brittany until he returned with Henry Tudor, who defeated Richard III at the Battle of Bosworth and was crowned Henry VIII. On his return, he gave thanks

by building the small chapel at the spot where he threw his hat.

The walkers will be reunited with the swimmers at Cotehele Quay, where stories of your adventures can be swapped over a hot chocolate, or something a bit stronger. Incidentally the old lime kilns make excellent changing rooms after your swim and are conveniently located right next to the café, which is run by the National Trust.

If you have the energy left, the main house at Cotehele is also worth a visit. The magnificently preserved Tudor house hasn't changed much over the centuries and while walls may not be able to talk, the volunteers will be happy to share the stories and legends.

The family built Cotehele between 1458 and 1565 to complement their main residence at Mount Edgcumbe; second-home owners existed in Cornwall, even back then. The family treated the property as a play-house and a historical talking point, keeping the Tudor features intact as a nostalgic reminder of the 'good old days'. The formally planted terraces, medieval stewpond and dovecote are also well worth exploring.

The house and quay were also used as filming locations in Trevor Nunn's 1996 film adaptation of *Twelfth Night*. And talking of Christmas, the house is a fantastic place to visit during December, when you can marvel at the spectacular garland that hangs the entire length of the Great Hall. Flower seeds are planted in February, and around 30,000 dried flowers are used to create the Christmas decoration. It takes the gardeners and volunteers two weeks to create every November and attracts thousands of visitors each December. However, even with the promise of a log fire in the Great Hall afterwards, we are not sure we would recommend doing the river swoosh in the winter!

1 From the car park, walk towards the quay past the Edgecombe Tea Room on your right and walk along the road where you drove in. At the fork, turn left for Plymouth, following the road as it bears around to the right.
0.2 miles

2 Where the road bends to cross Cotehele Bridge on your left, leave it and carry straight on, taking the path into the woods with the stream on your left.
0.2 miles

3 You reach a fork, where you turn left and cross the stream on the wooden bridge to visit the mill.
0.1 miles

4 From Cotehele Mill, retrace your steps to the fork in point 3. Turn left and keep left, passing the weir on your left.
0.5 miles

5 At the road, cross straight over past Newhouses cottage on your right and follow the lane down.
0.1 miles

6 You reach a five-bar gate on the right with a small stone stile to the left. Cross the stile and follow the path here up through the wood. Be sure to take this first permissive path, not the public footpath a little further to the left, which will take you in the wrong direction. Carry straight on at a junction where the path bends round to the left.
0.3 miles

7 Go through a wooden gate into a field to walk up between the cherry trees. At the end of the field, go through the gateway and turn left along a track and past a cream house on the left called Newton Farm.
0.2 miles

8 Turn right just after Newton Farm and then turn right into the lane opposite Rose Park House. Continue uphill on the lane.
0.2 miles

9 At the T junction at the top of the lane, go straight across over the stile and follow the public footpath along the left-hand edge of the field.
0.2 miles

10 At the end of the field, go through a wooden gate next to a five-bar gate. You can see Prospect Tower off to the right and you could divert along the field edges to visit it, returning to this point. Carry on walking along the left-hand boundary of the field. About half-way down head across to the right, aiming for a stile you will see just beyond two telegraph poles.
0.2 miles

11 Go over the stile into the woods, turn right then immediately left and walk down a steep hill to the bottom.
0.2 miles

12 At the stream, turn right following the yellow arrow.
0.1 miles

13 You reach a fork with a sign to Cotehele House on the right. Go left here, past Wood Cottage on the left, with the stream on your right. The track becomes a road hugging the river on your right, which you follow all the way into Calstock, going under the viaduct. It ends in a T junction where you turn right and then right again almost immediately, heading down towards the water past the Tamar Inn.
0.8 miles

14 At the slipway, swimmers can get in the water and simply swim back to Cotehele Quay. Walkers need to retrace their steps from here to the fork in point 13. At point 13, turn left following the Cotehele House sign and ascend through the woods with the river on your left.
1 mile

15 You reach a fork; take the left-hand path and start the descent back down towards the quay.
0.1 miles

16 You pass Calstock Lookout on your left, with wooden railings and a commanding view of the river and viaduct.
0.1 miles

17 Take a look around Chapel-in-the-Wood on your left, before following the path back to the car park.
0.3 miles

Prussia Cove